About this book

Havana is the capital of Cuba. There are more than 3 million inhabitants there. The date of establishment is 1519. Havana is the biggest cultural city in Cuba. There is the Old Havana, and the more modern districts of Vedado and Miramar. Old or downtown Havana is full of culture with its ancient villas, squares, fortresses, churches and monuments that will keep visitors happy and intrigued. Additionally there are a lot of retail spaces commercial centers, office buildings, hotels, bars and clubs, and even a Chinatown. Old Habana in located in the Centro Habana district. It is the smallest of the 15 municipalities of Havana, but has the highest population density.

The Miramar area has few tourist attractions and more known for its location of government services and where diplomatic residences are concentrated. The Vedado district is noted for its local action. It is in the center of Habana with easy access to most other parts of the city including downtown Havana. Lodging is more than adequate with many hotels of all sizes from the likes of luxury high-rise hotels such as the Havana Libre ,Hotel Nacional de Cuba, and the Hotel Riviera Havana, to smaller ones including the more economical bed and breakfast style lodging of the popular casa particulars. Restaurants are plentiful as are other social activities. This is one of the few places in Havana where tourist and locals mix.

Cuba is truly an amazing place to visit. Upon first arrival, seeing the old buildings and architecture, and old 1950 classic American cars in full operation, was like entering a twilight zone or stepping back in time.

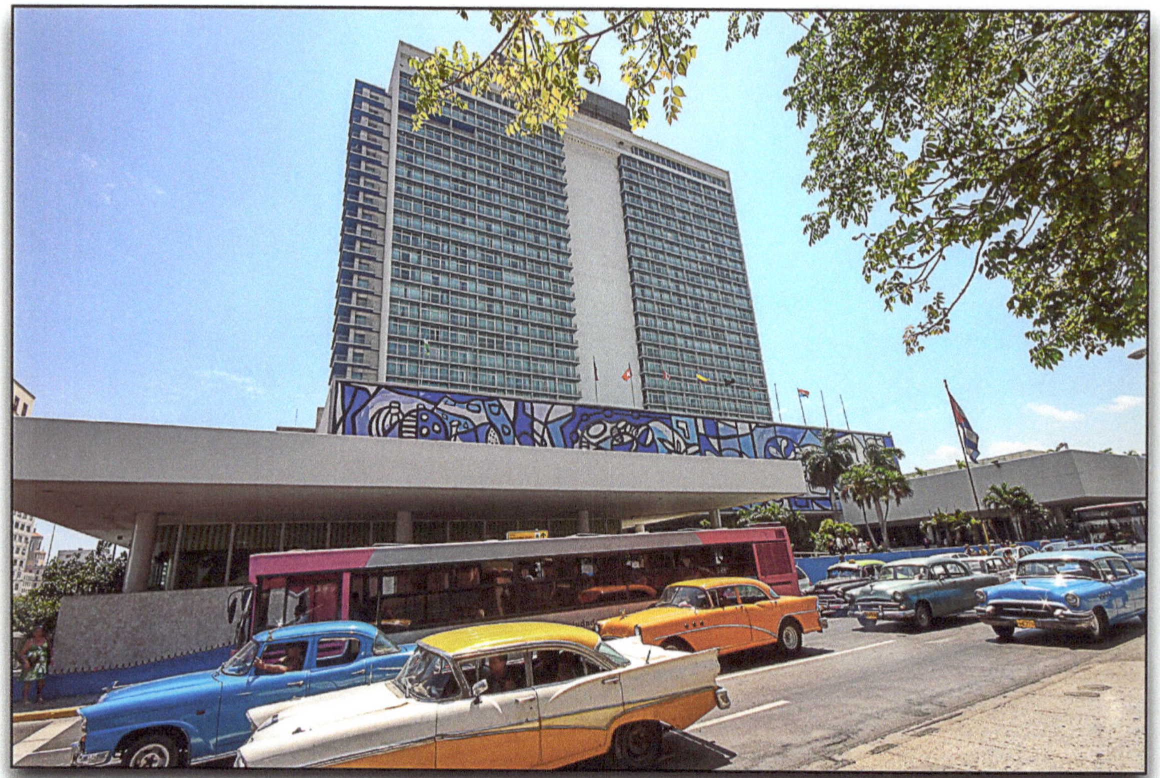

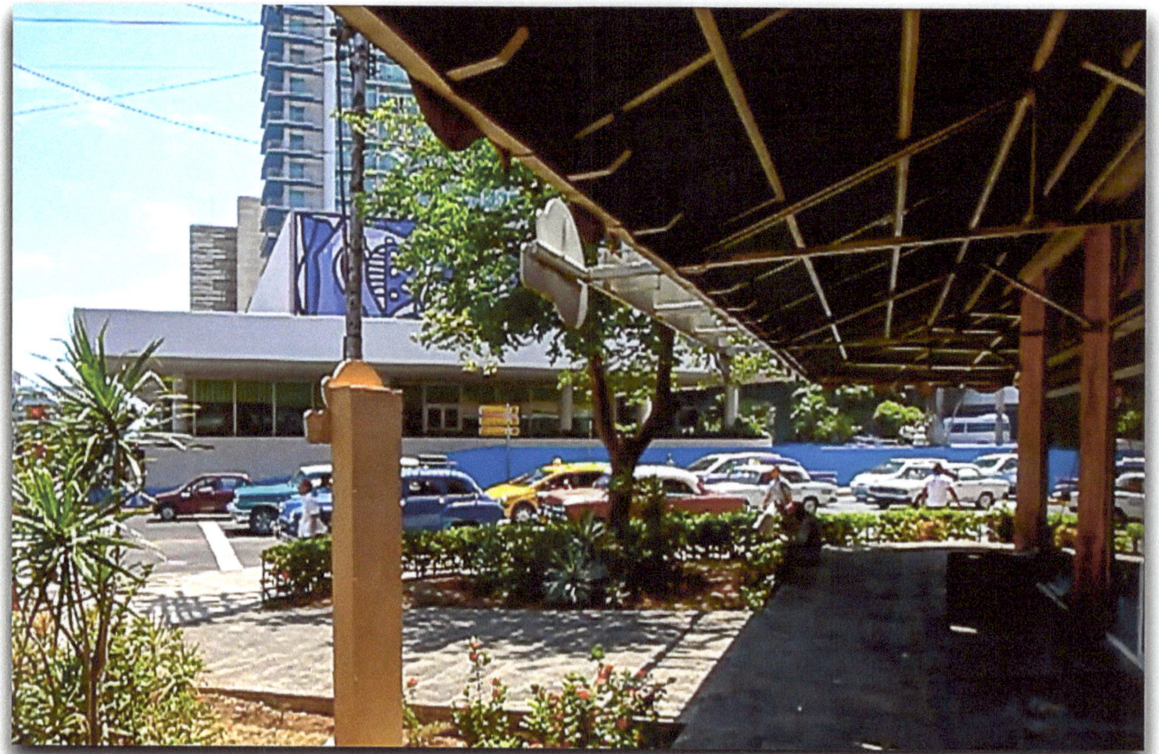

Watching the cars as they sit at stop signs or pass in front of the Hotel Habana Libra, and nearby intersections, is like watching an American classic car show. These drivers are not parading their cars however, they are on their way to work and other destinations at seven in the morning. Currently, the only way these cars stay on the road today is by using Cuban ingenuity to adapt household products and Soviet technology into these vehicles. They are seen throughout Cuba in abundance. Many are used for taxi cabs.

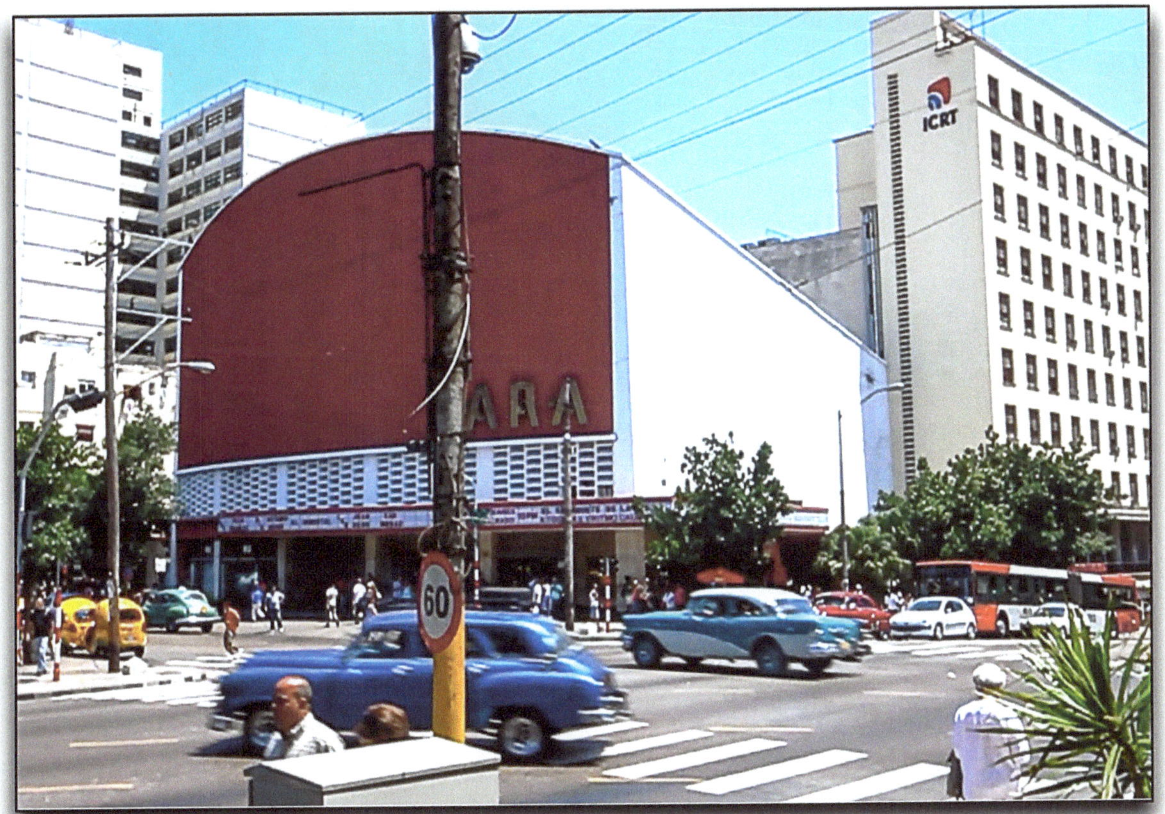
ICRT
60

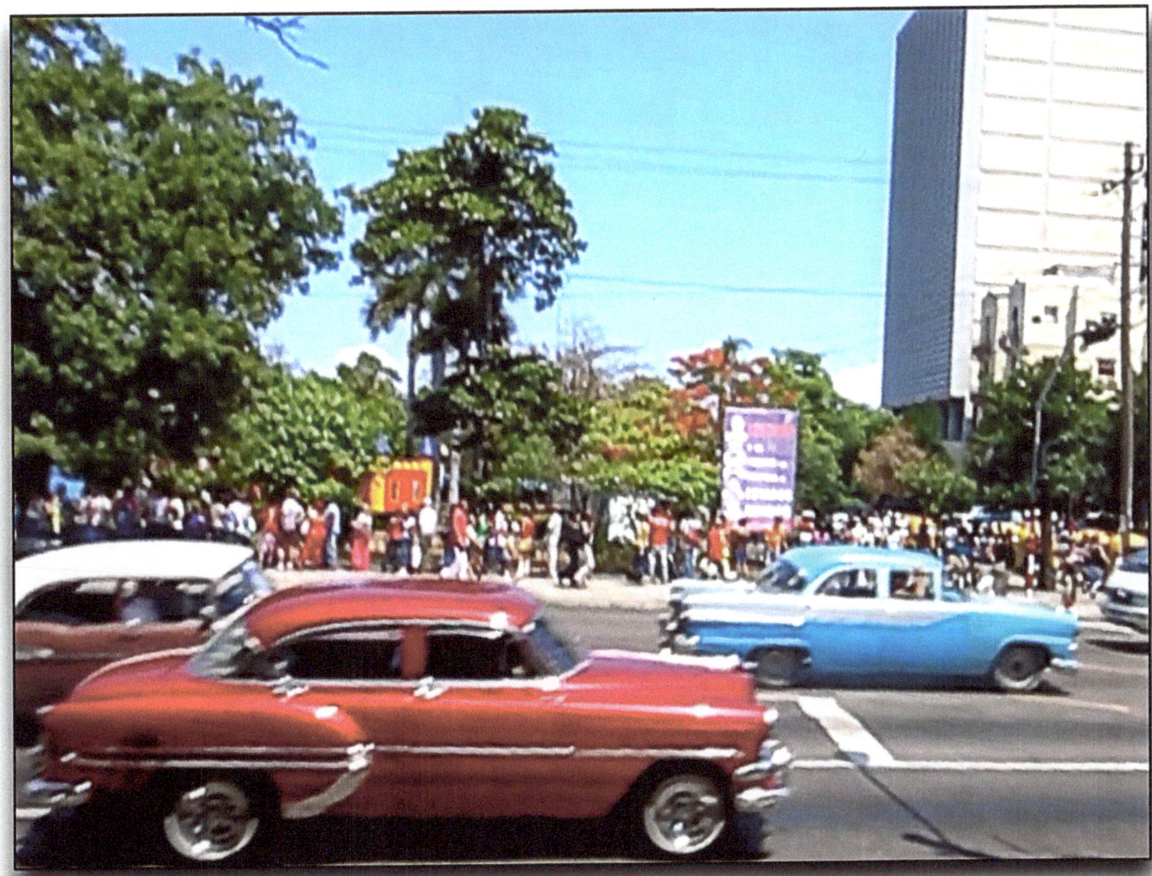

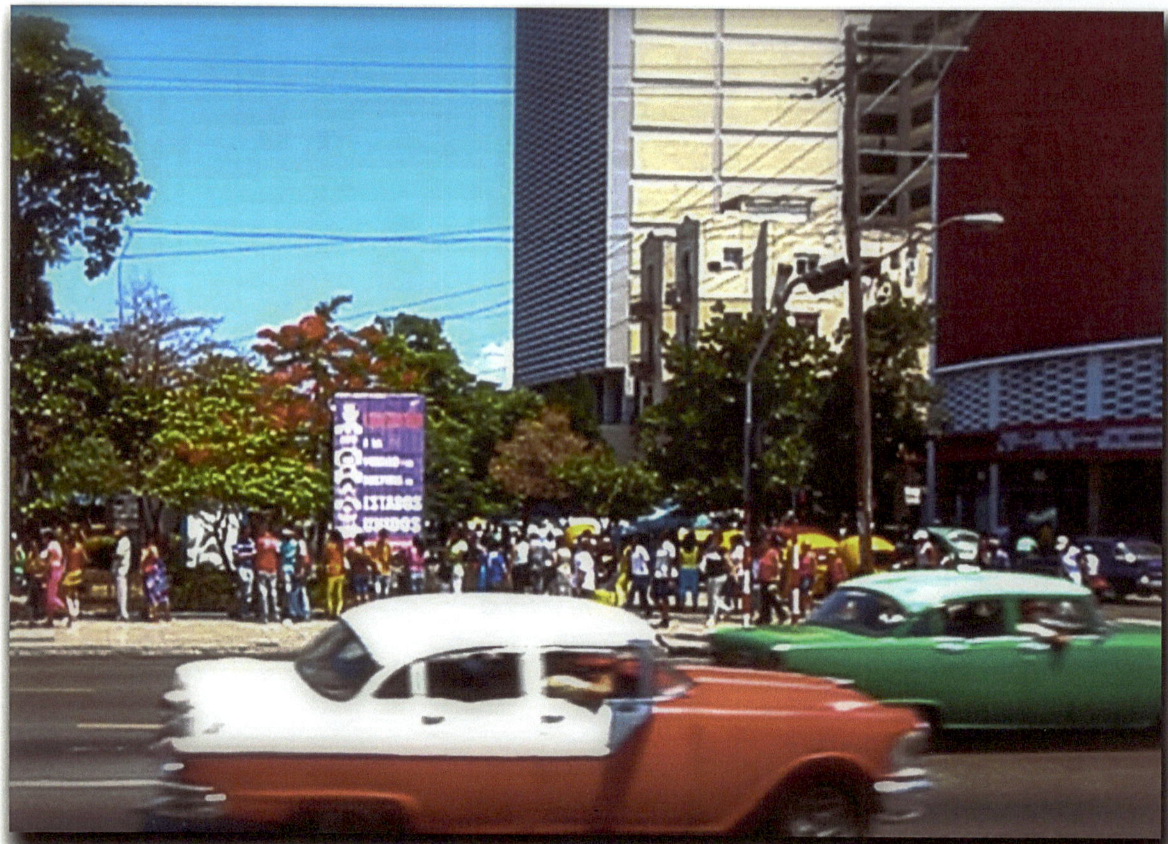
ESTADOS
UNIDOS

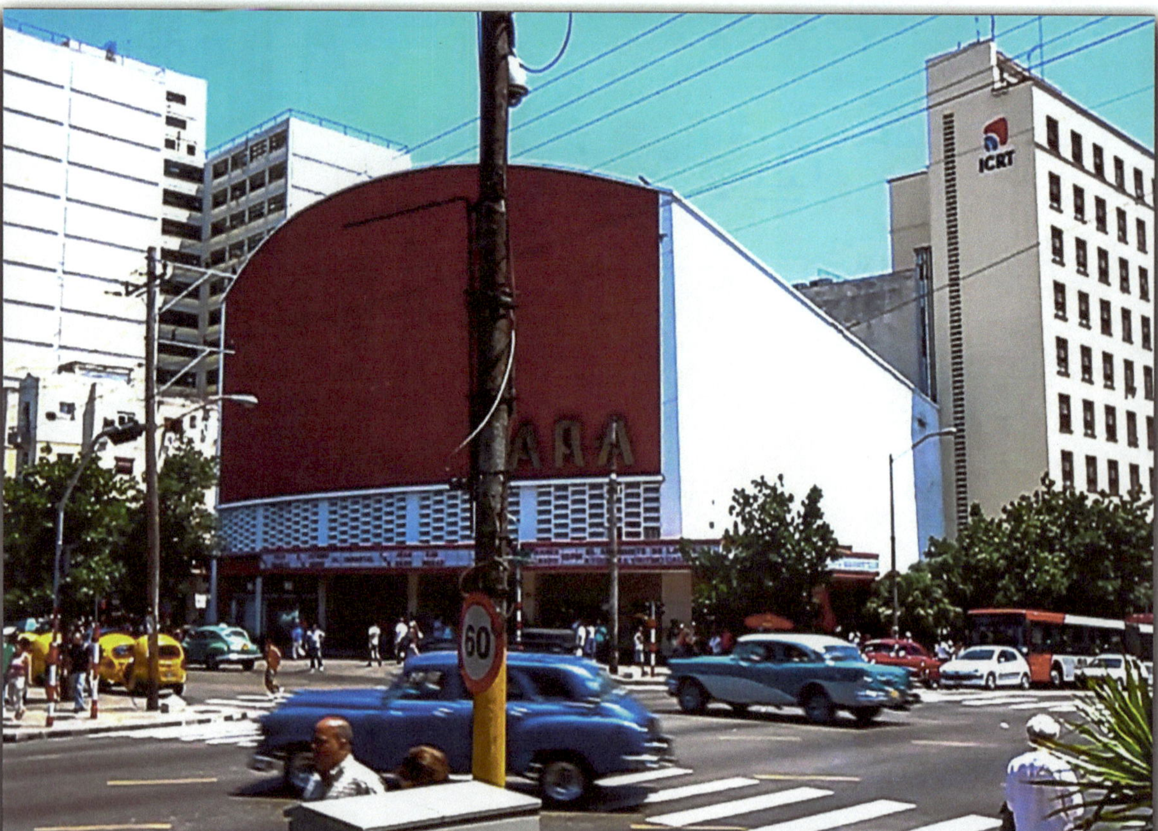
ICRT
60

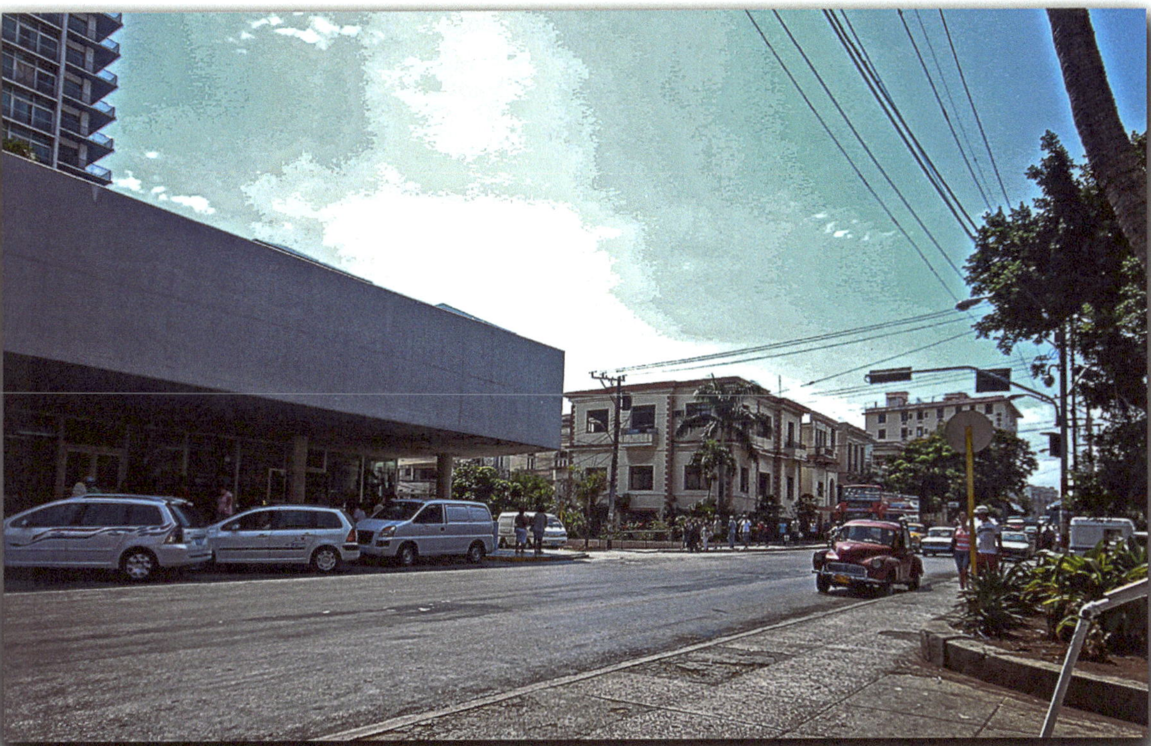

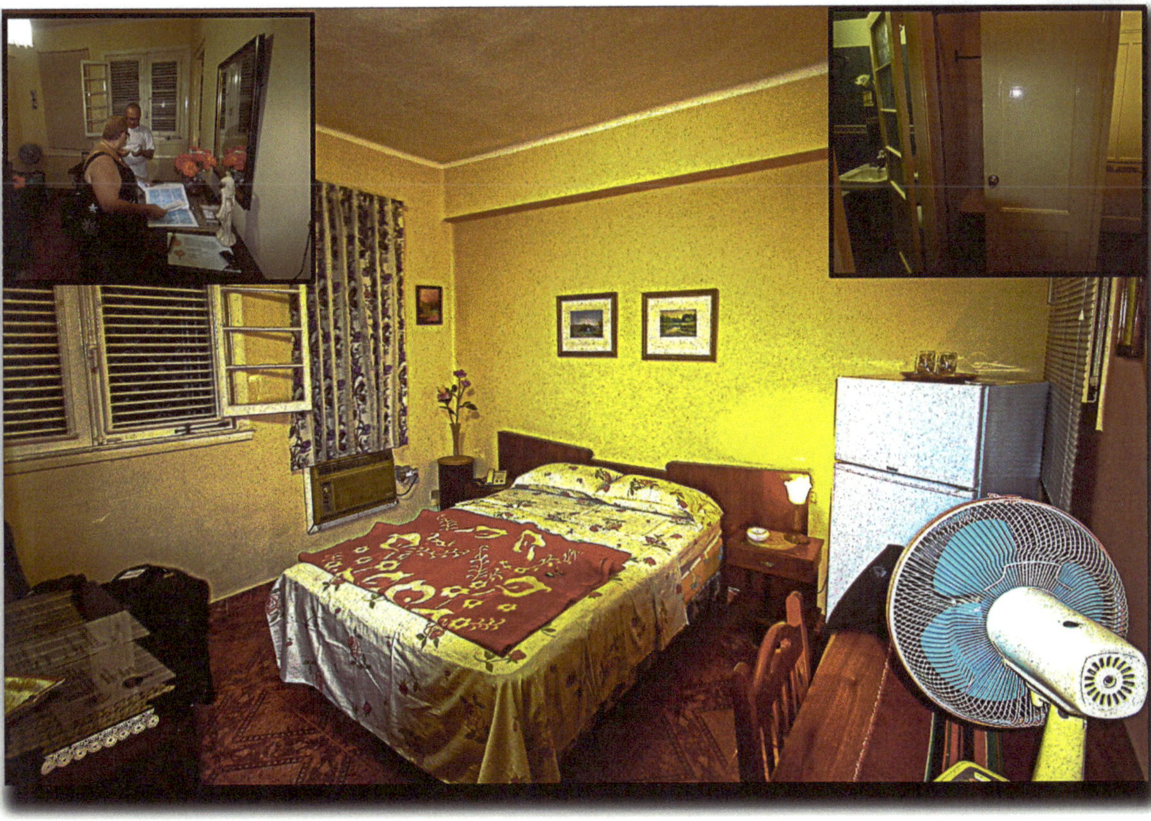

This is a typical Casa Particular in Havana. Lodging is a Bed & Breakfast style private room with full accommodation in a house with a Cuban family. Its secure. inexpensive lodging for the visitor and helps a Cuban family. The price can range from as little as 5-10 tourist dollars a night. This particular one is right across from the Hotel Habana Lebre where for a little fee you can have access their rooftop pool and other amenities, and enjoy the benefits of both worlds at little cost.

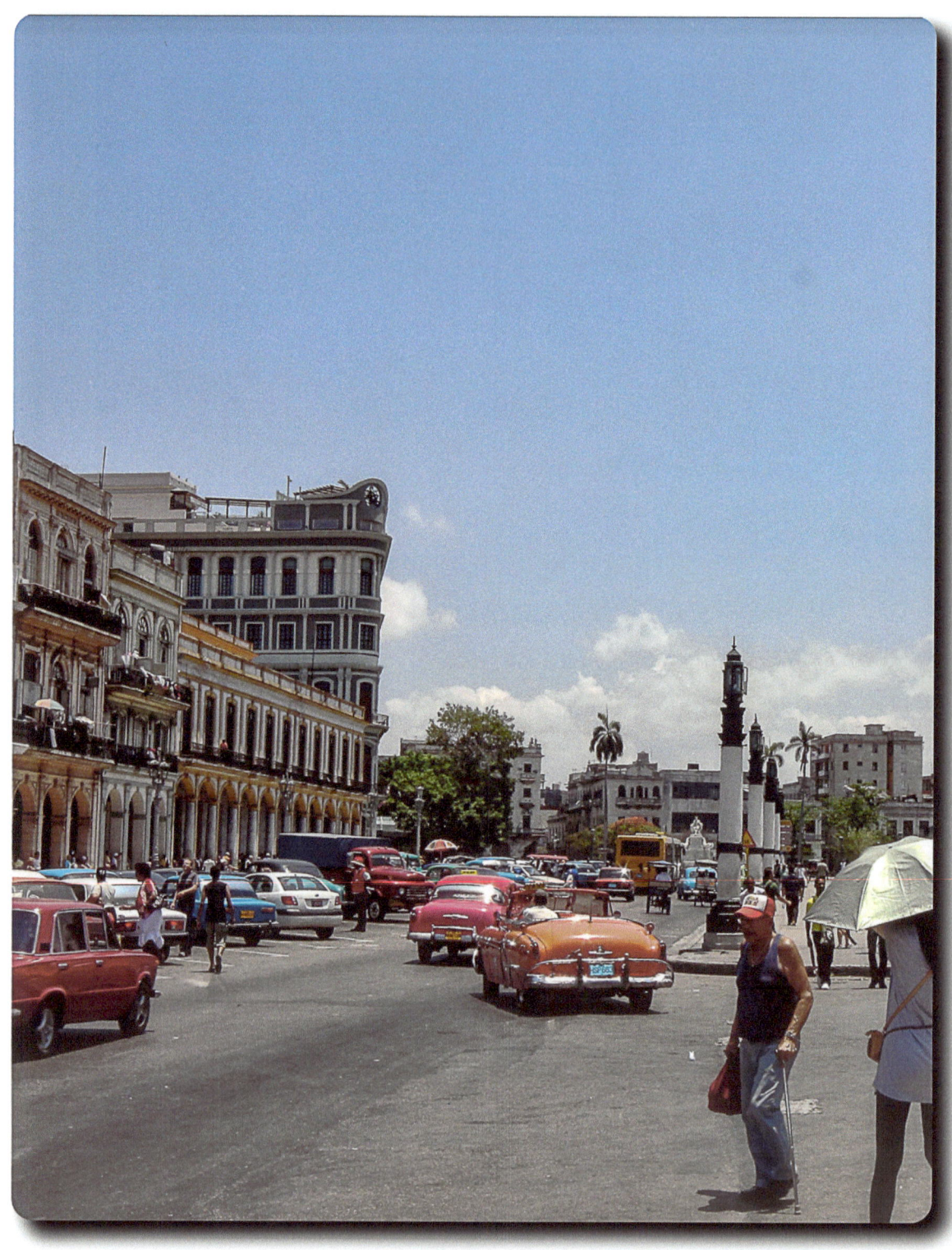

This is Downtown Havana, or Old Havana, as it is known. By adhering to its original design and urban layout it has maintained its overall sense of architectural and historical character. The urban plazas are surrounded by many buildings of the old original Spanish architectural designs with narrow streets lined with popular and traditional styles. When tourist visits Havana Cuba, this is where they head and mingle most. The people, the buildings, the music, the history, and the food make it truly an amazing place to visit.

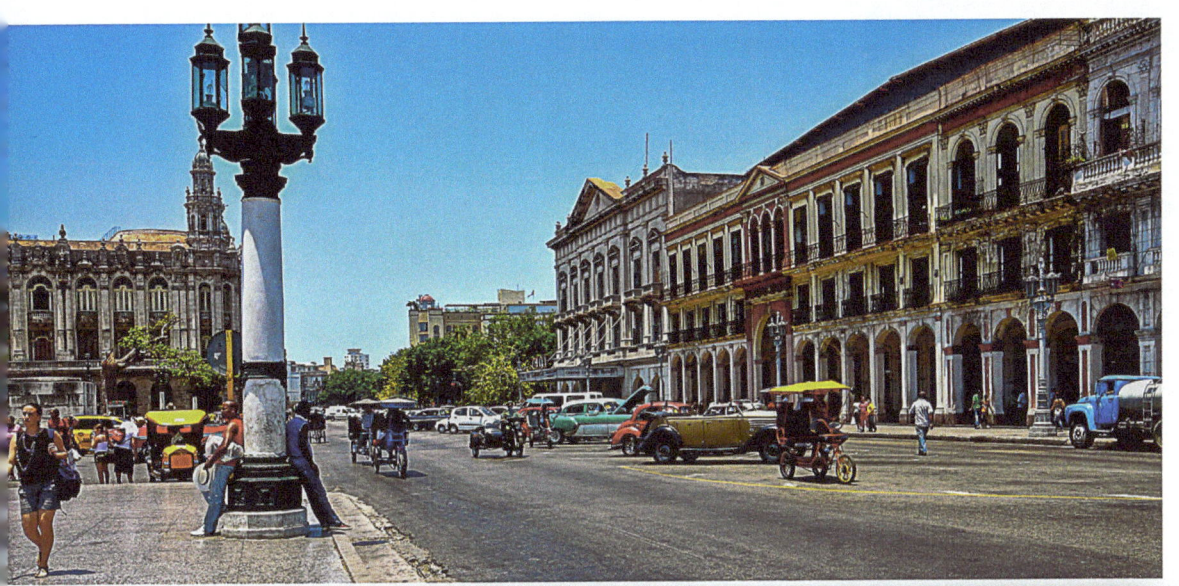

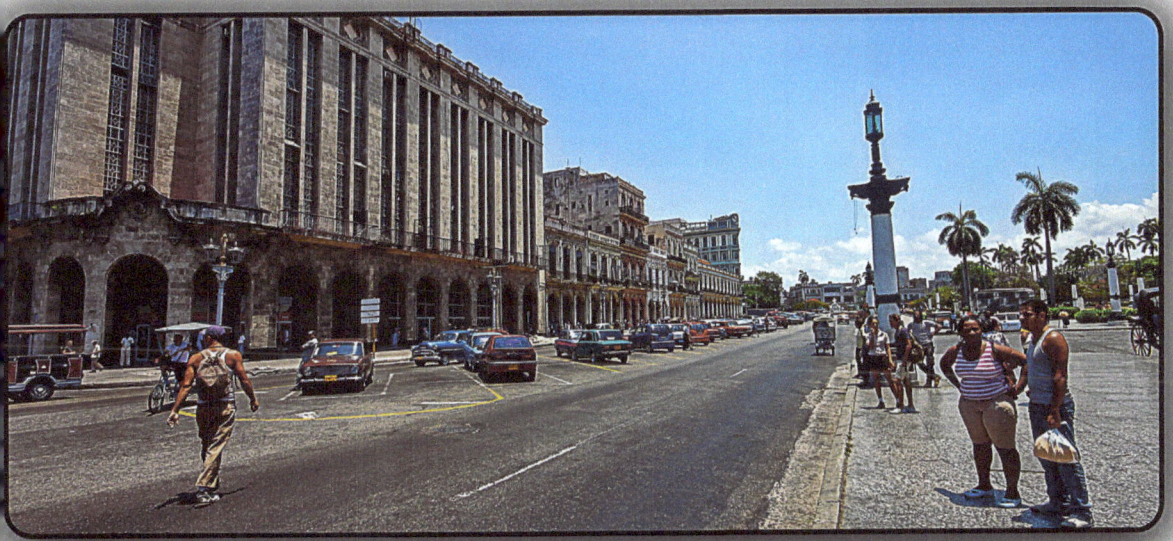

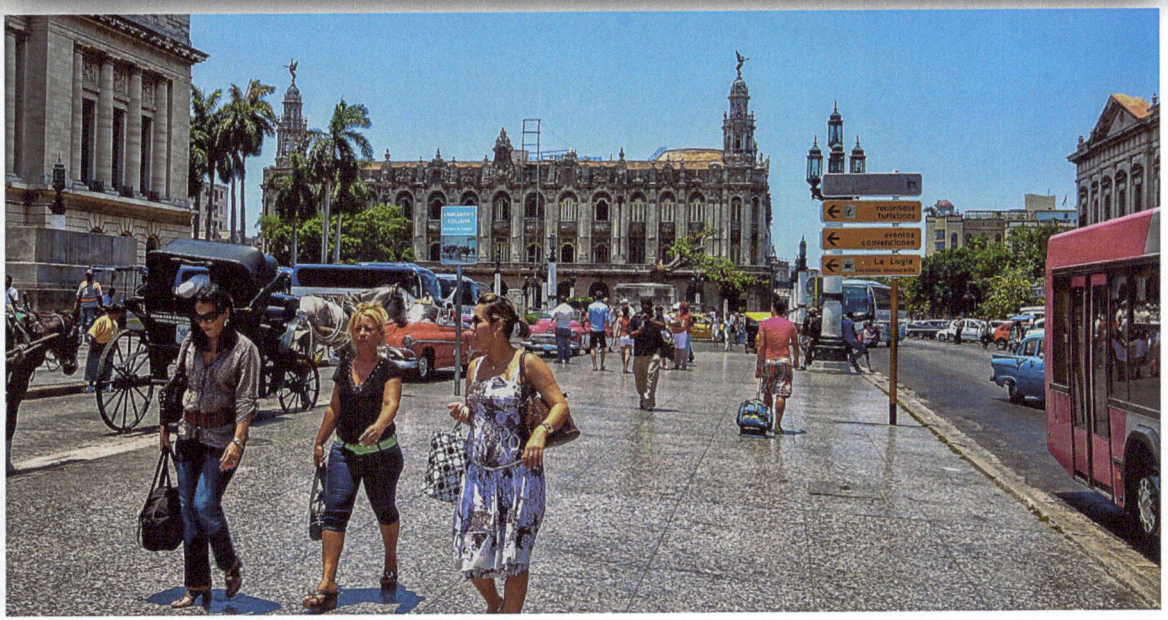

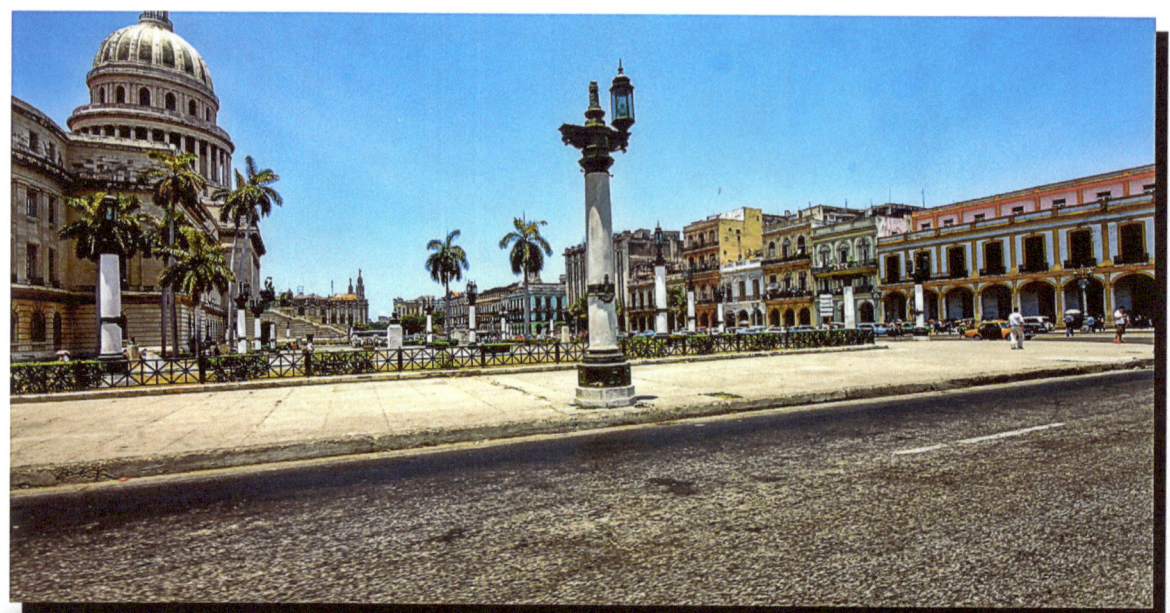

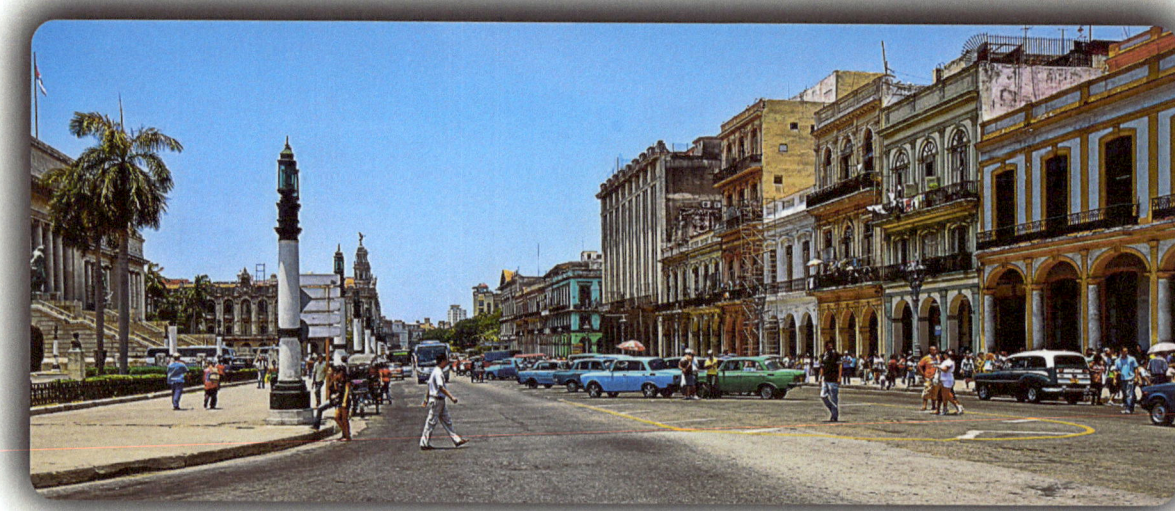

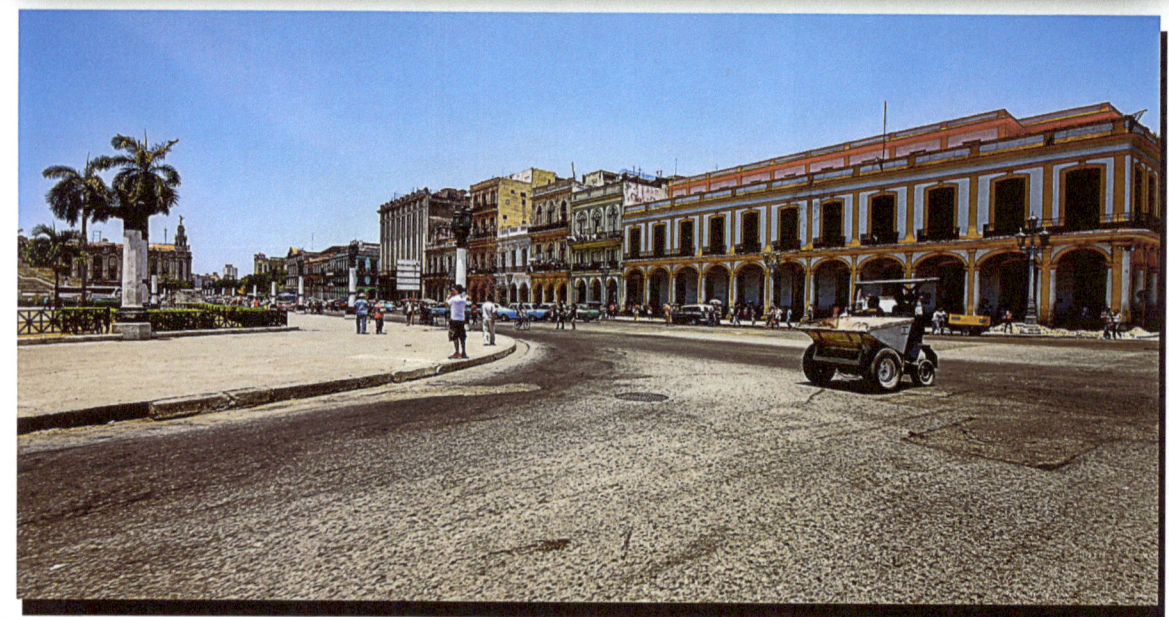

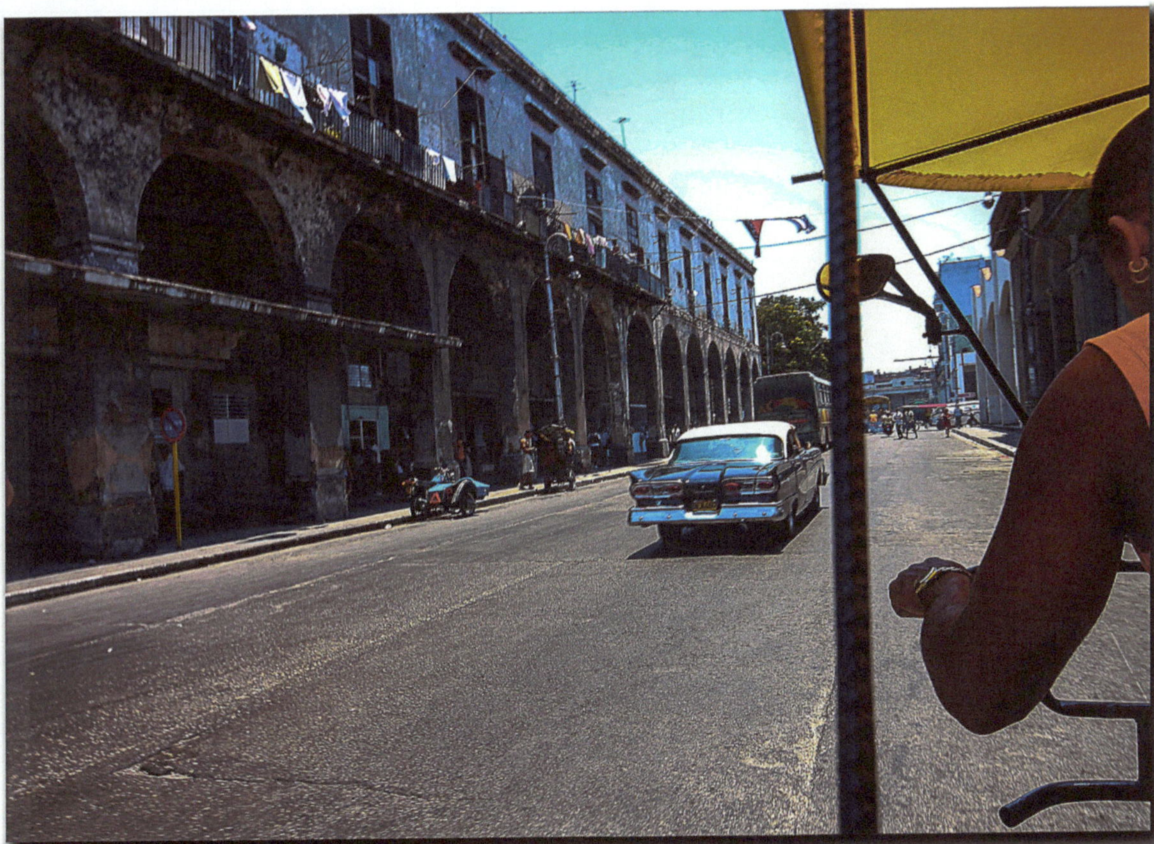

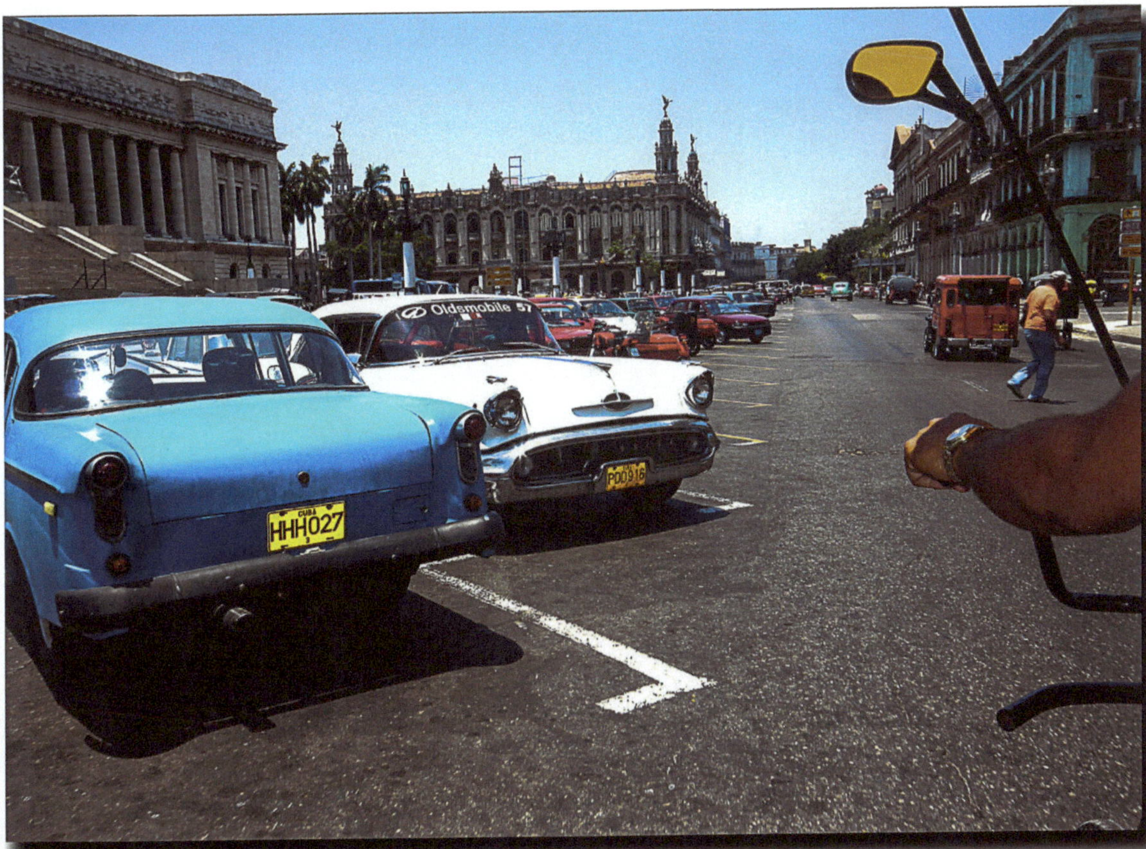
Oldsmobile 57
HHH027

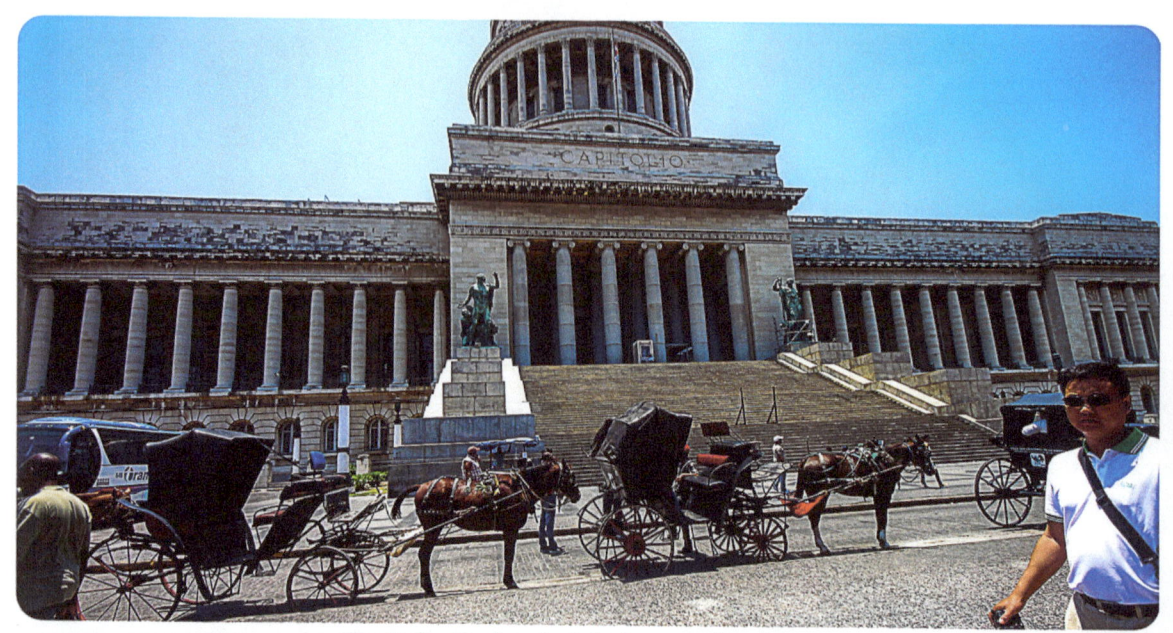

Capitolio Nacional: Cuba's capital building

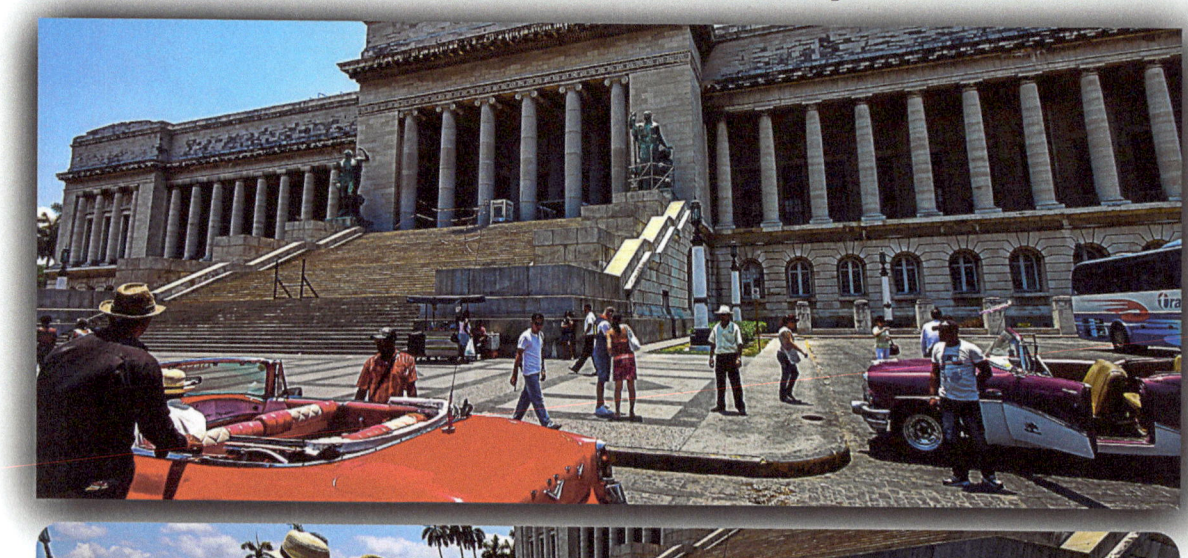

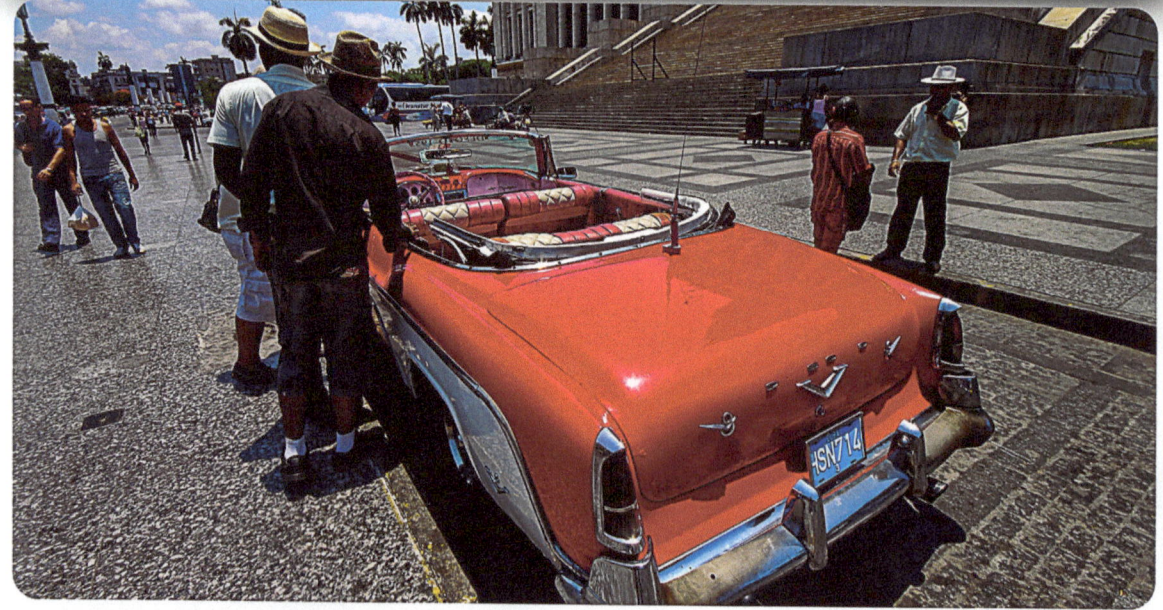

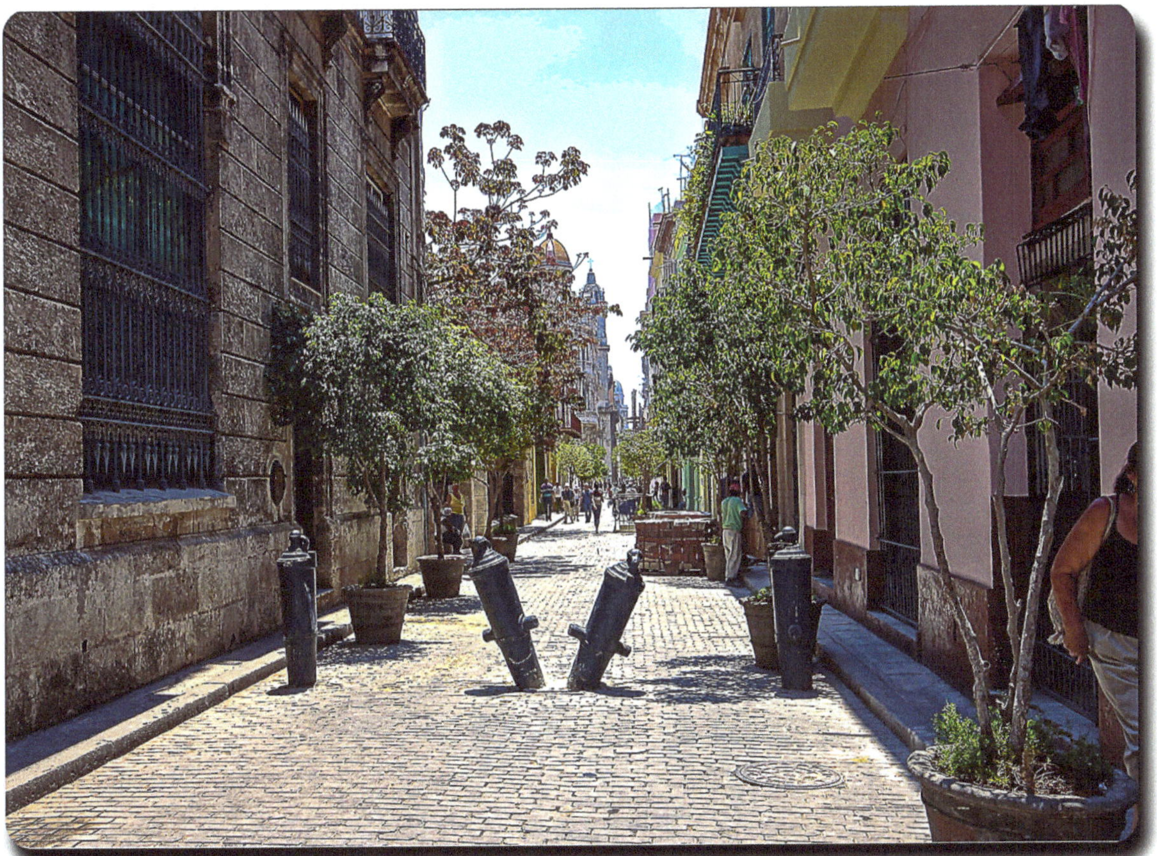

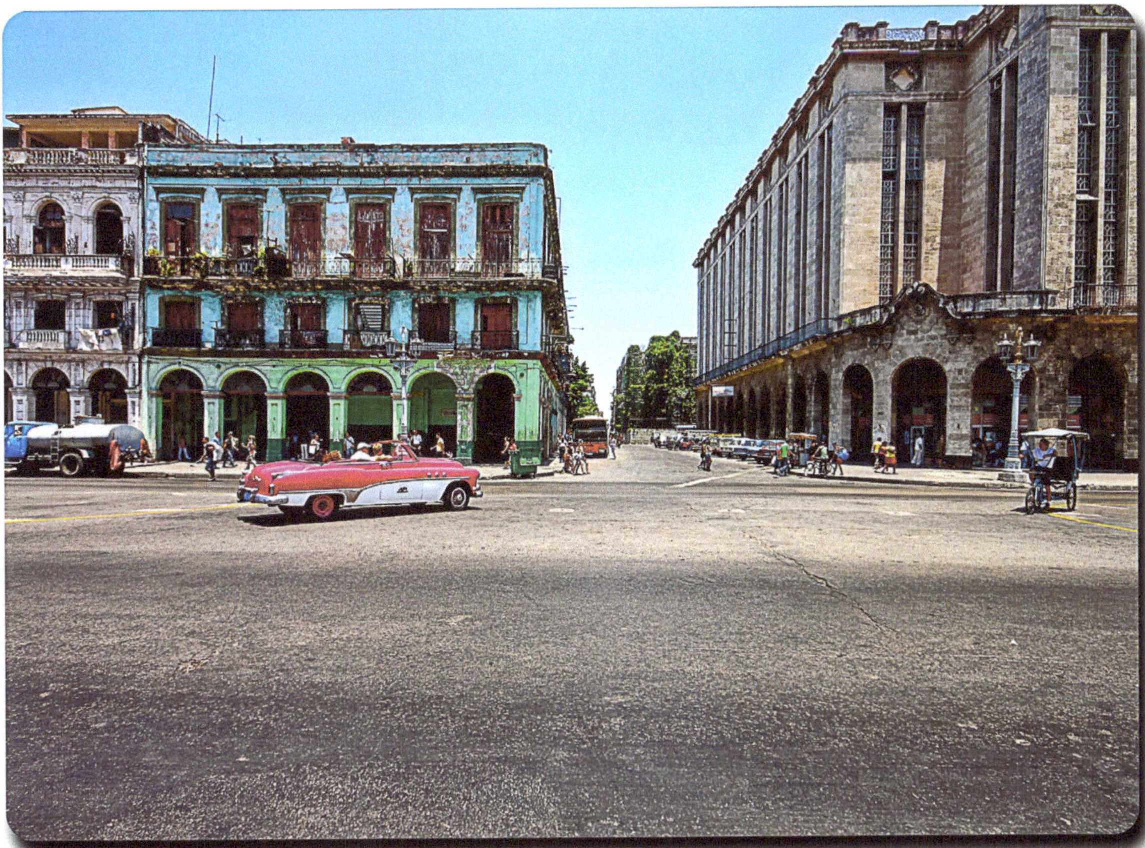

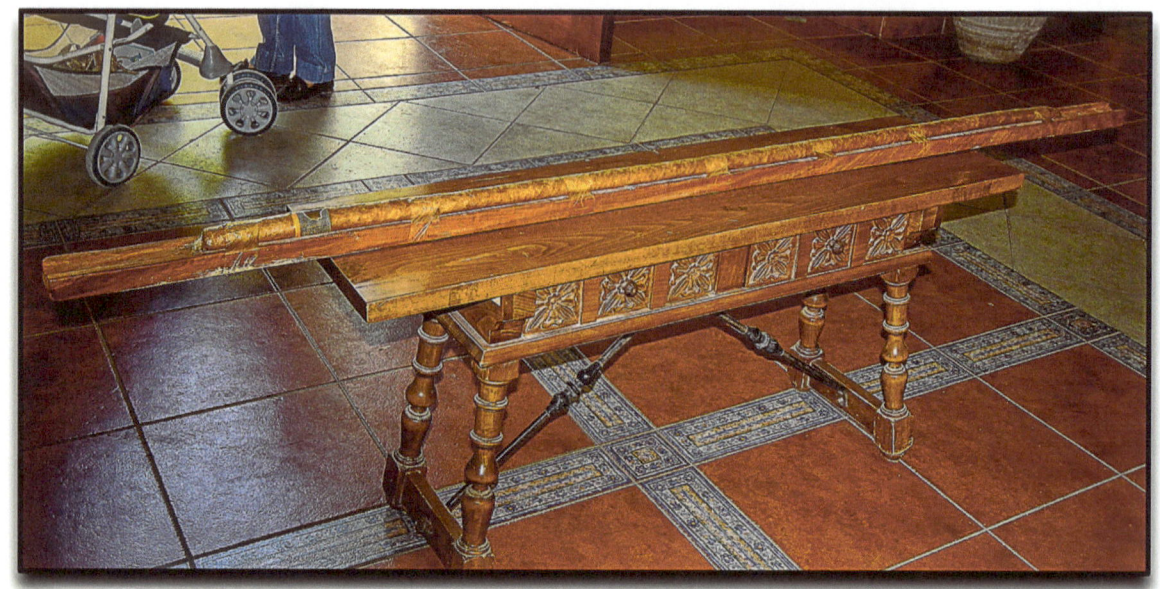

And here you have..on display....the largest cigar in all of Cuba

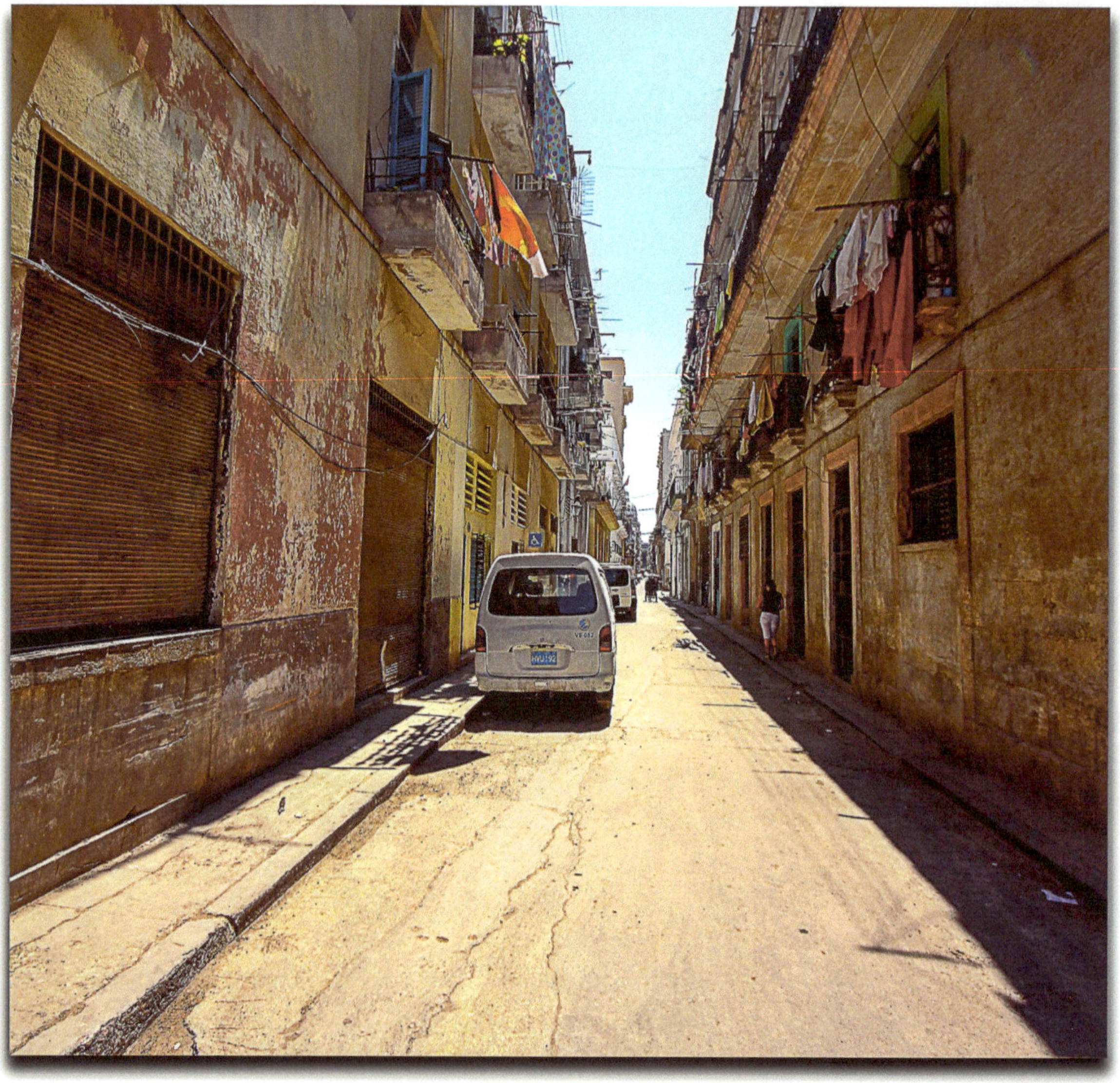

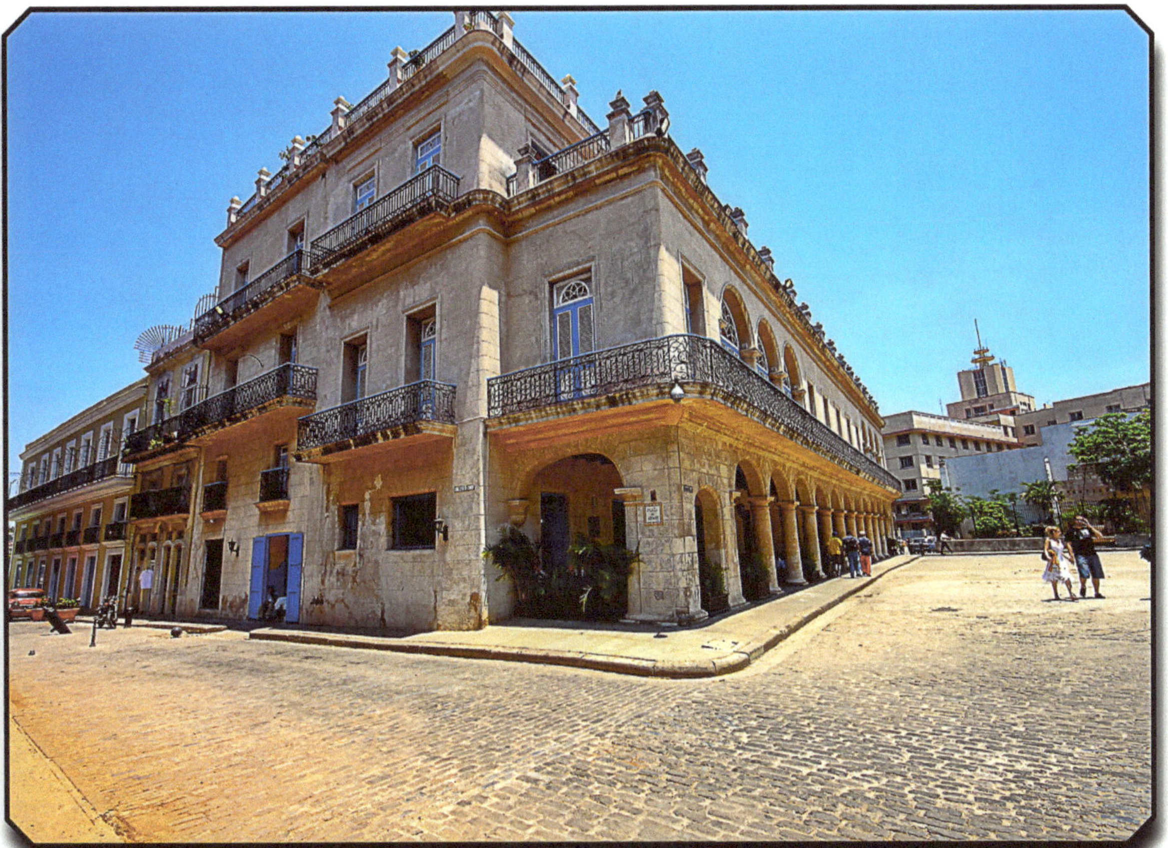

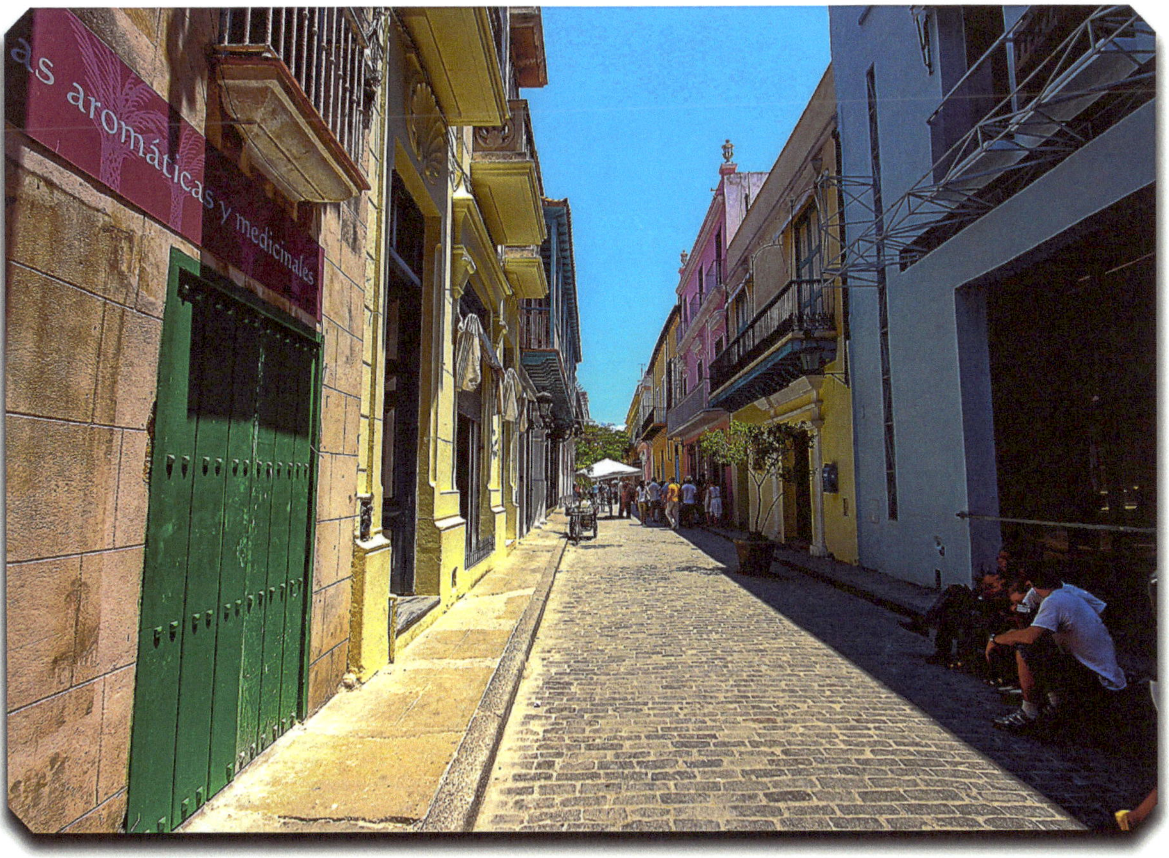

as aromáticas y medicinales

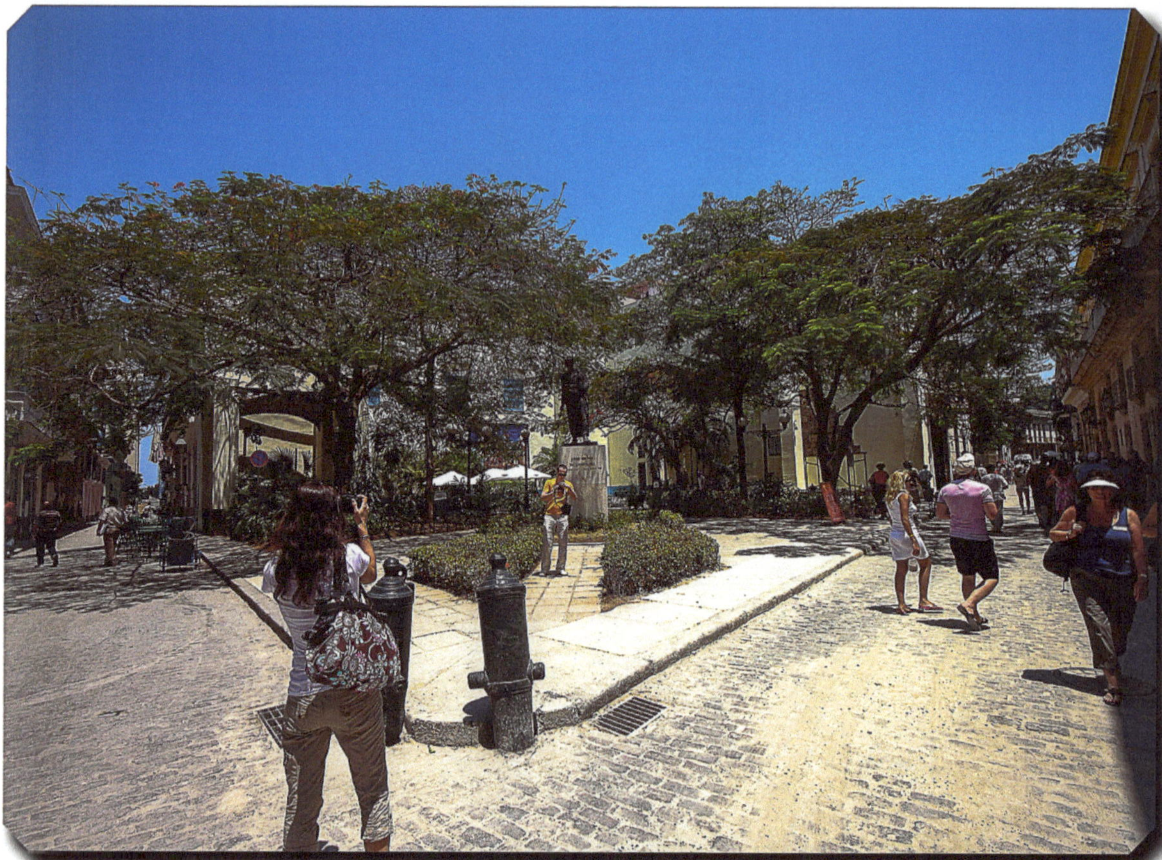

Plaza de Armas

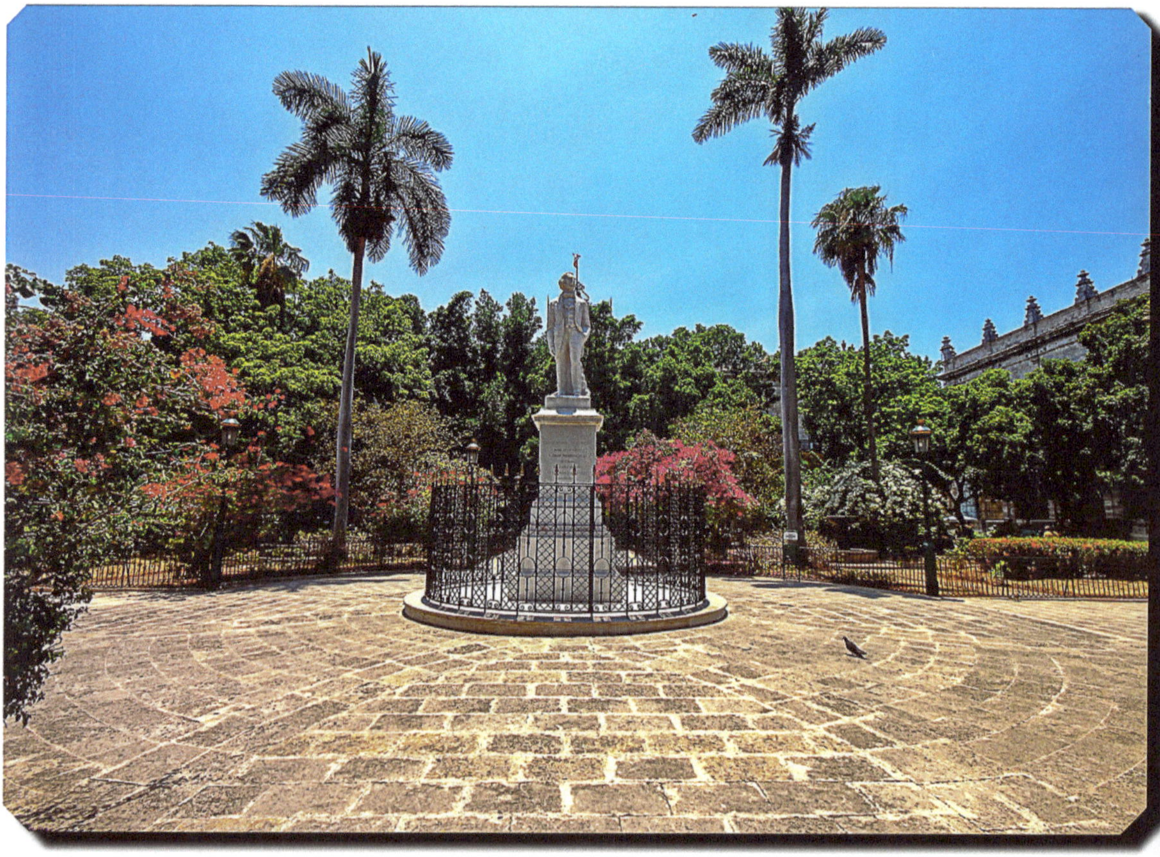

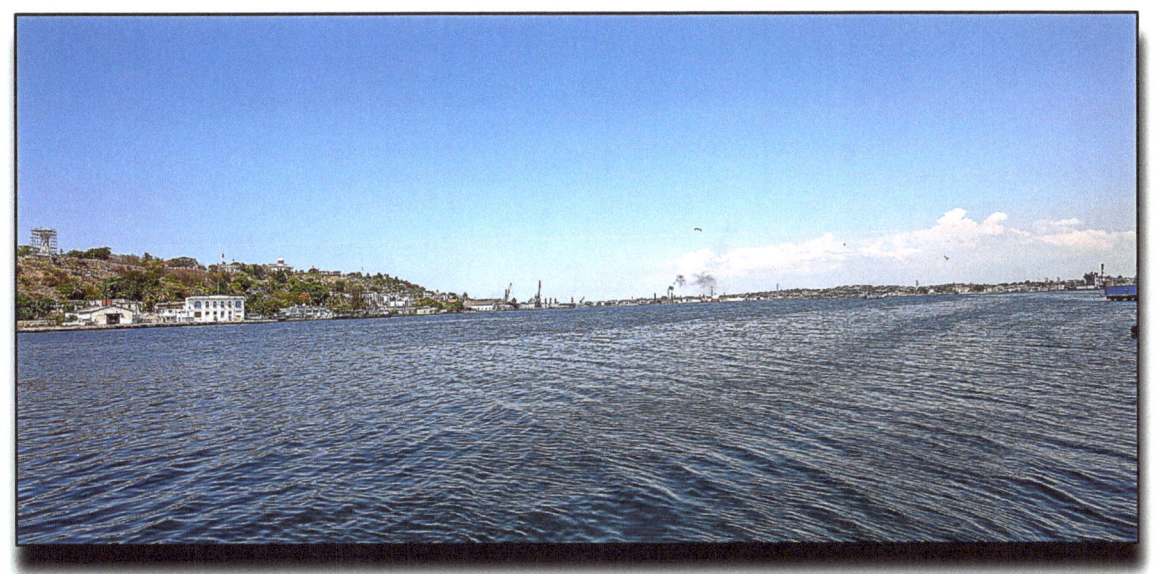

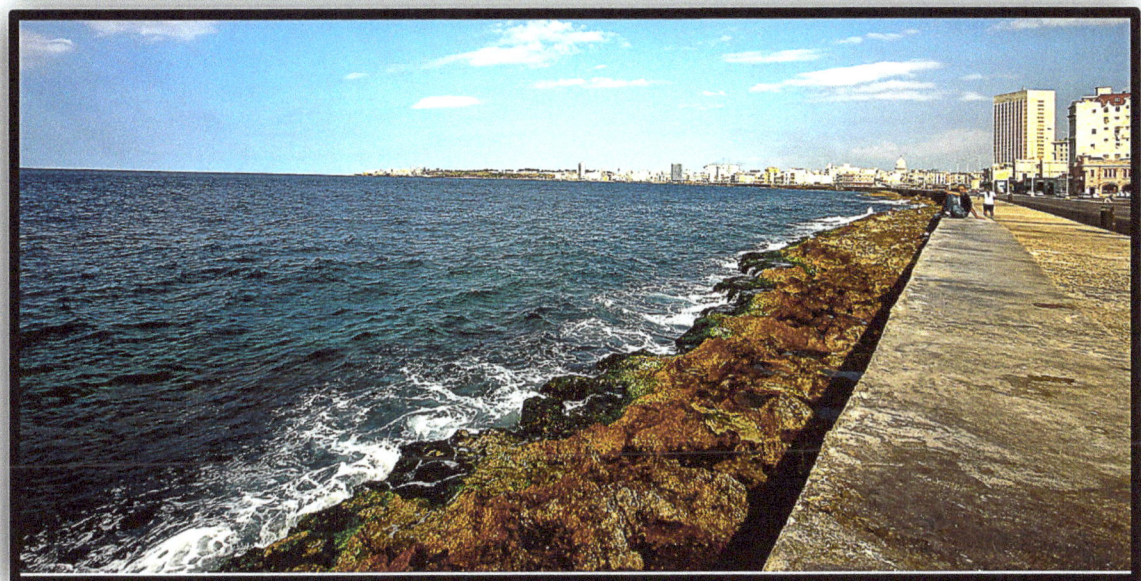

Havana's El Malecón, is a long esplanade that curves alongside the waters shaping Havana's skyline.

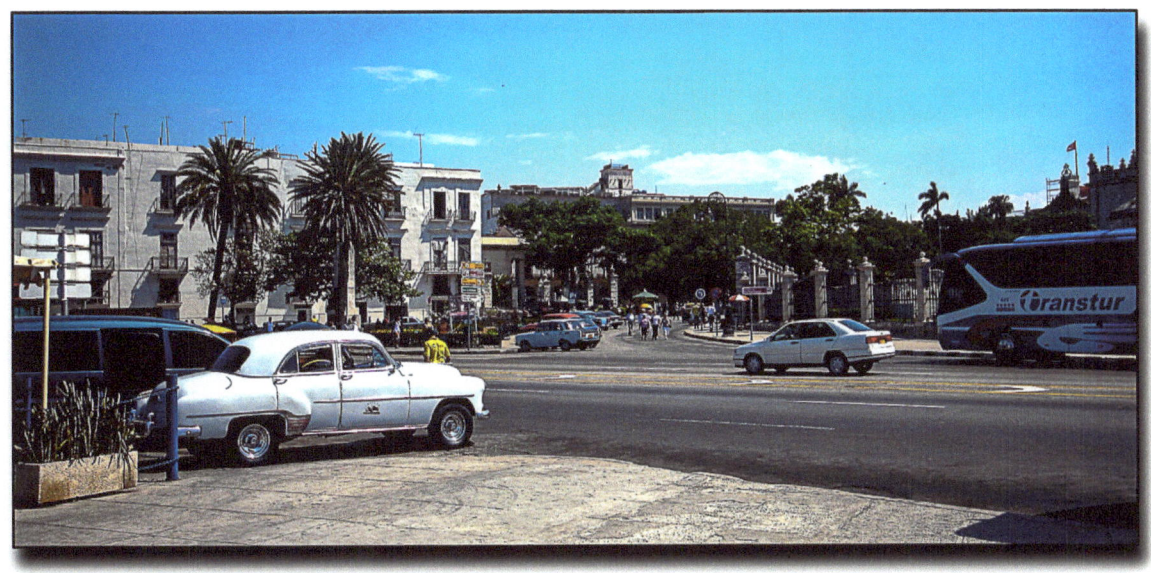

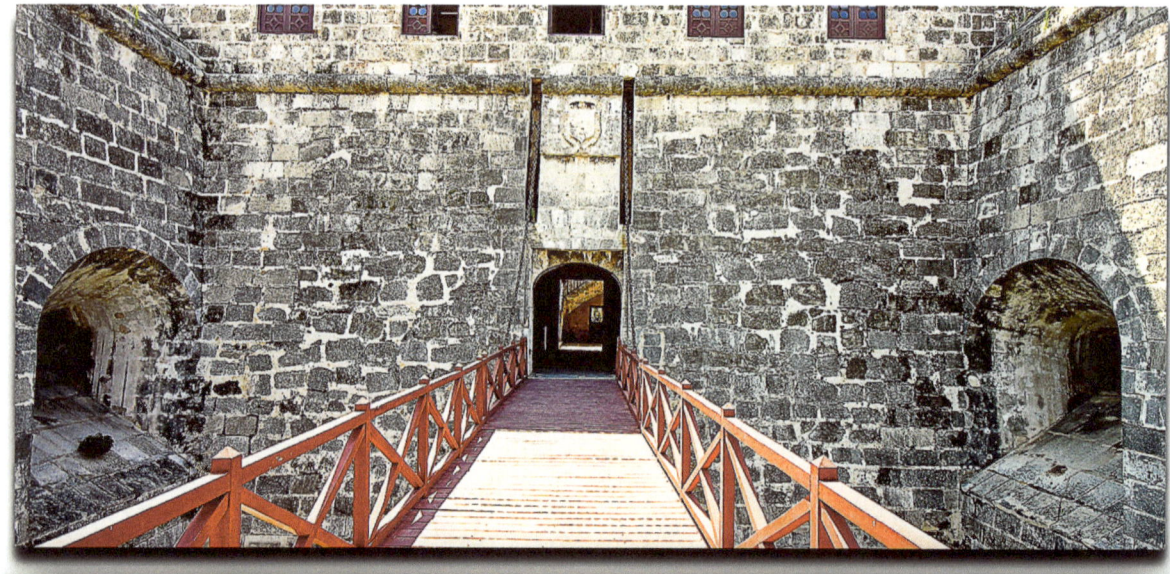

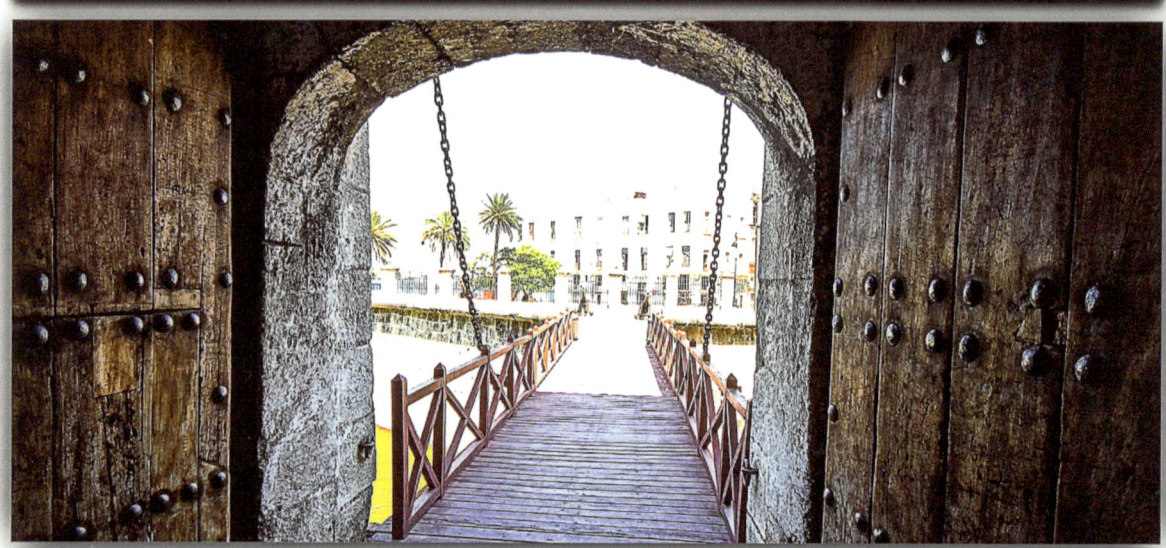

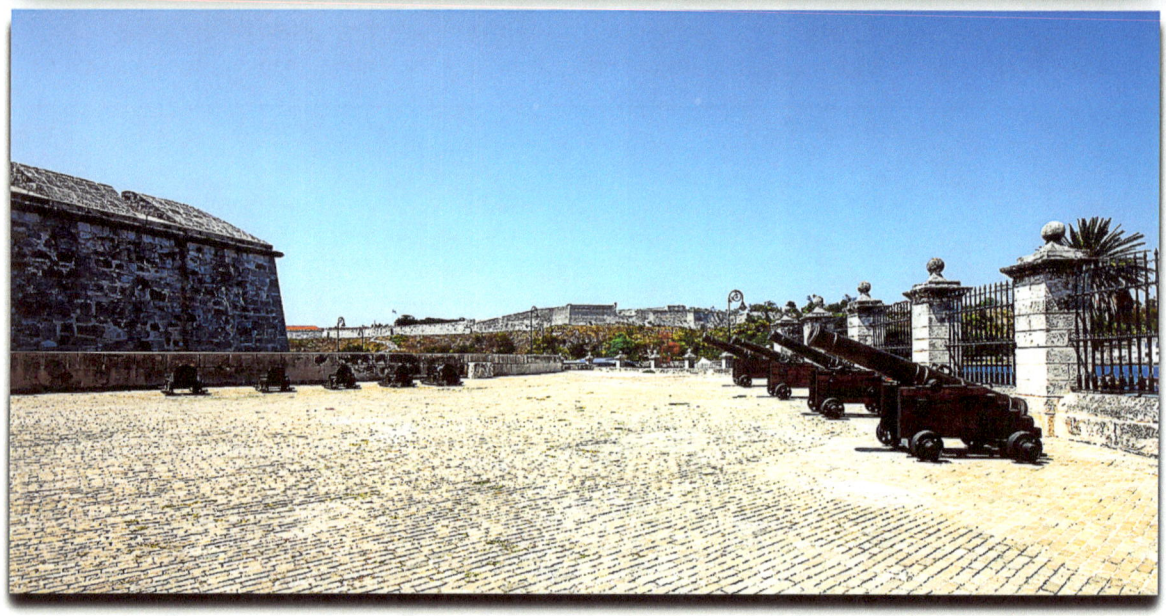

Fort San Salvador (Castillo De San Salvador De La Punta)

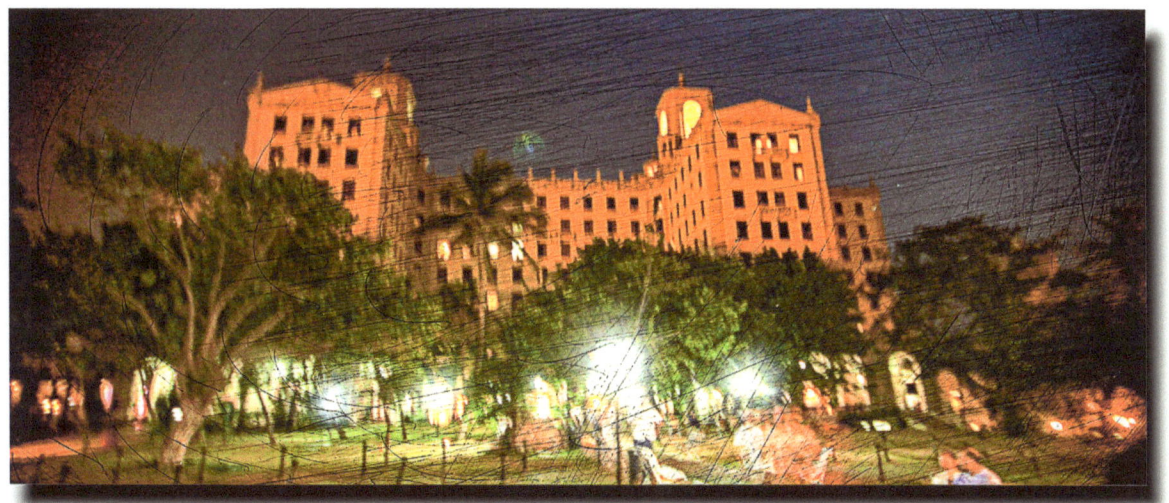

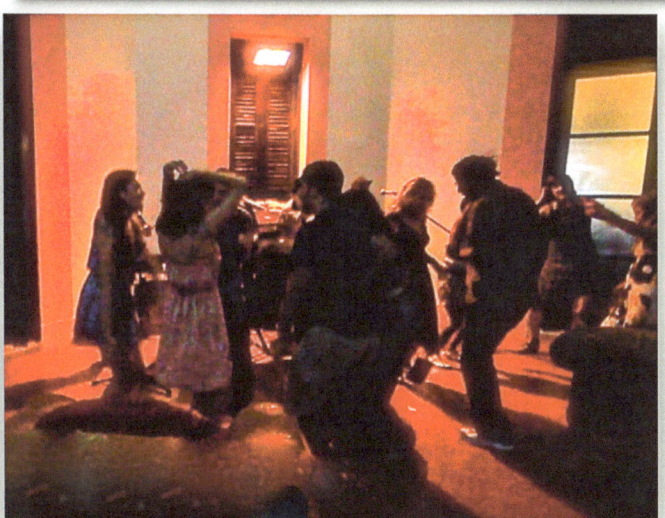

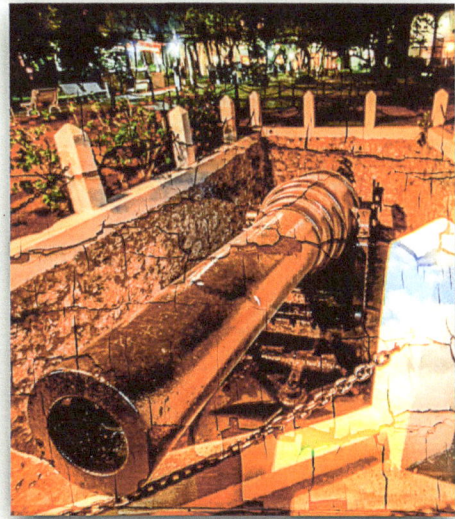

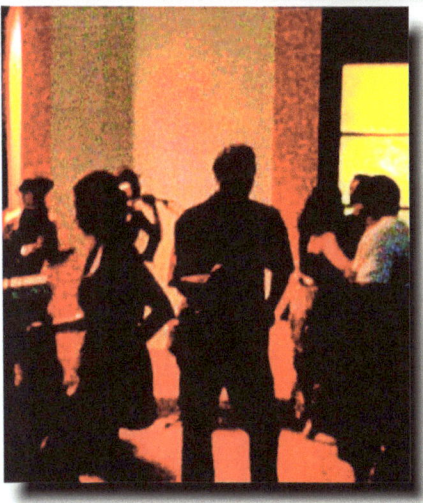

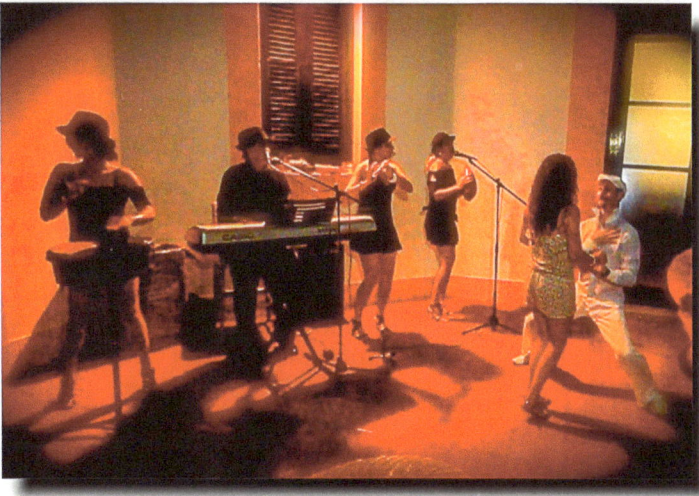

Night life at the Hotel Nacional de Cuba. Hotel Nacional is a a World Heritage Site and a National Monument. During its heydays, especially prior to being confiscated during the cuban revolution, it hosted illustrious guests from Winston Churchill to Ava Gardner, including the most popular celebrities in all aspects of society. The hotel's popularity attracted mobster Meyer Lansky, a Polish American organized crime lord who turned a part of the hotel into a lucrative las Vagus style restaurant, bar, and luxurious casino.

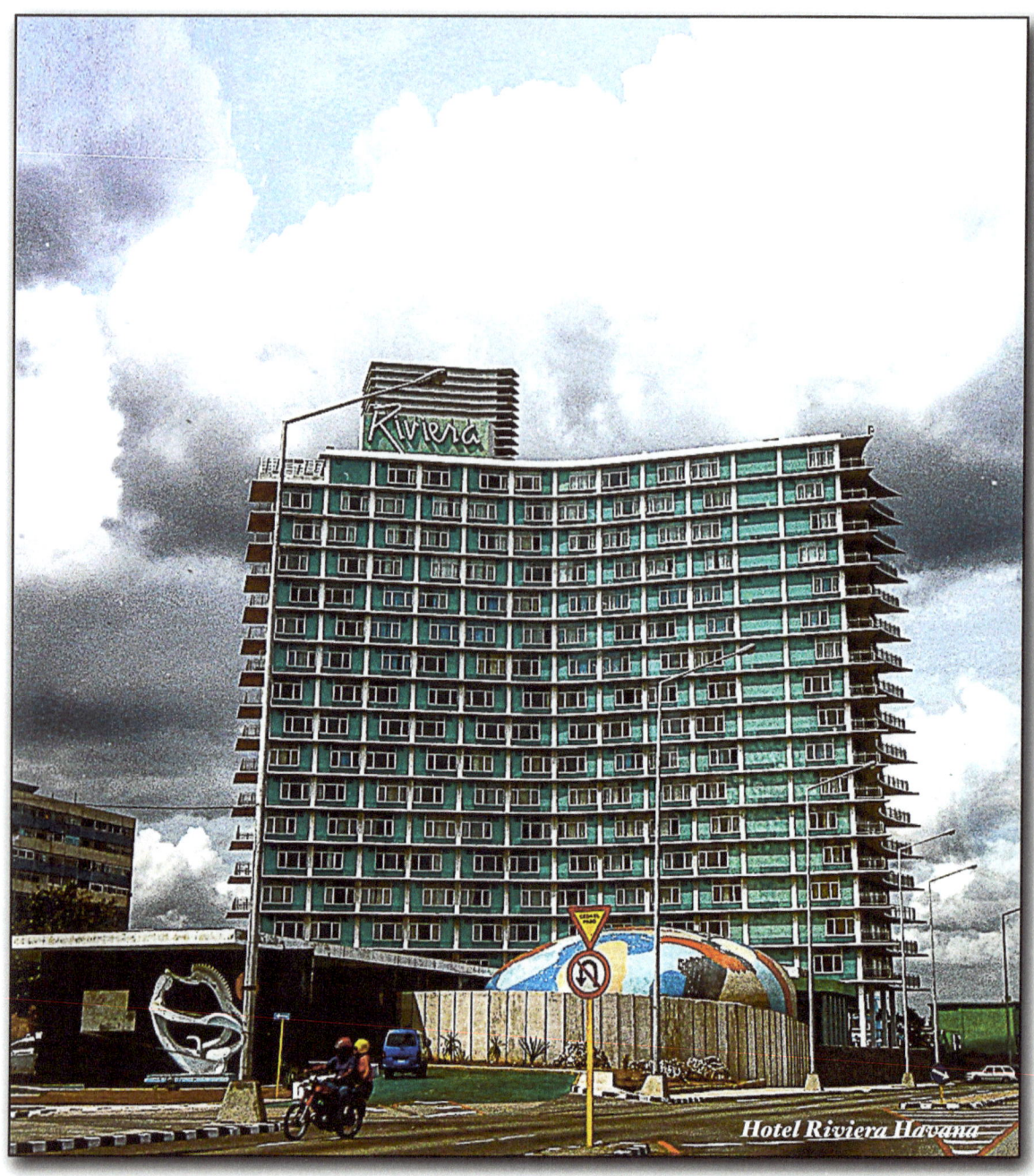

Hotel Riviera Havana

Prior to the Cuban Revolution (1953-1959) the ambitions of organized crime went over the top. Cuban president Fulgencio Batista had antagonized the Cuban population by forming lucrative links to crime lords and mobsters with the likes of Meyer Lansky and Moe Dalitz, and allowing American companies to dominate the Cuban economy. Eventually this lead to the Cuban Revolution, a successful armed revolt conducted by Fidel Castro.

Figuring he could escape US gambling laws and FBI scrutiny, Mobster Lansky had high ambitions to turn Havana into a Las Vegas style environment of large lavish hotel casinos such as the Havana Libre (Hotel Free Havana), originally built as the Havana Hilton; the Hotel Nacional de Cuba which he owned a part of; and the Hotel Riviera Havana which he had built with collaborating investments of other mobsters.

In 1959, when Lansky heard that Castro preferred executing gangsters to deporting them, he quickly charted a plane to the Bahamas escaping with nothing more than his life. In the year following success of the revolution, Castro nationalized all the island's hotel-casinos and outlawed gambling. Today, with the exception of casinos and gambling, most of these hotels are restored and retain their splendor, excellent features, and amenities to attract visitors and the tourist trade.

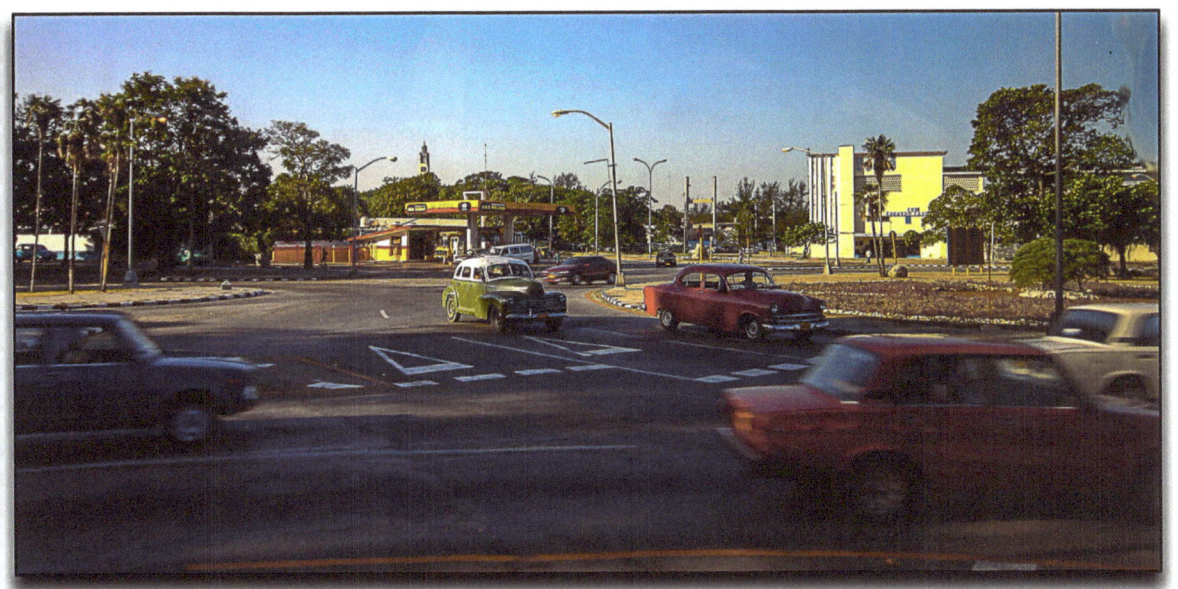

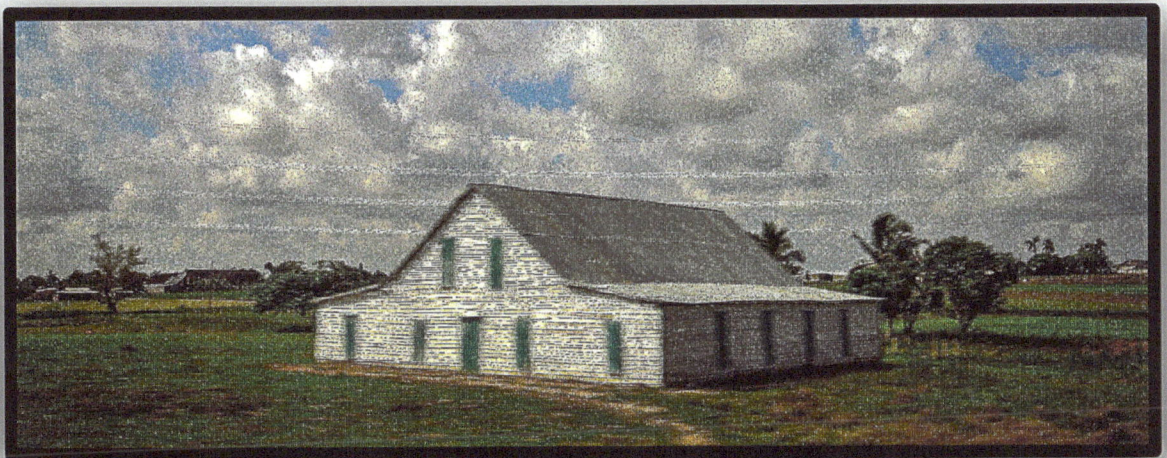

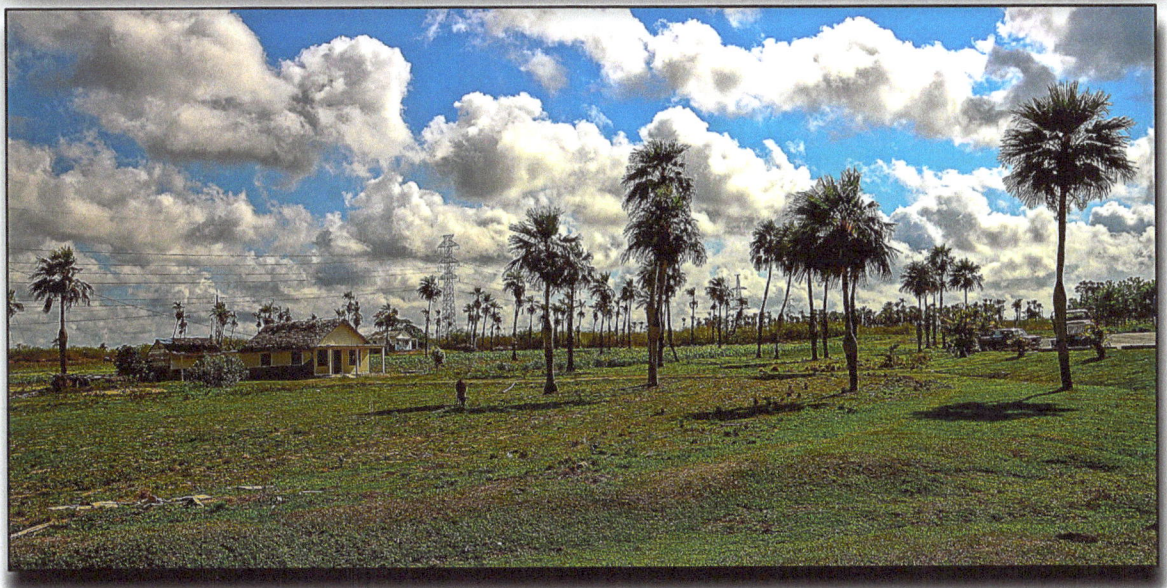

Beautiful countryside in route to Viñales Valley. The valley is located in Cuba's Pinar del Río province where much of Cuba's prime agricultural sites are found.

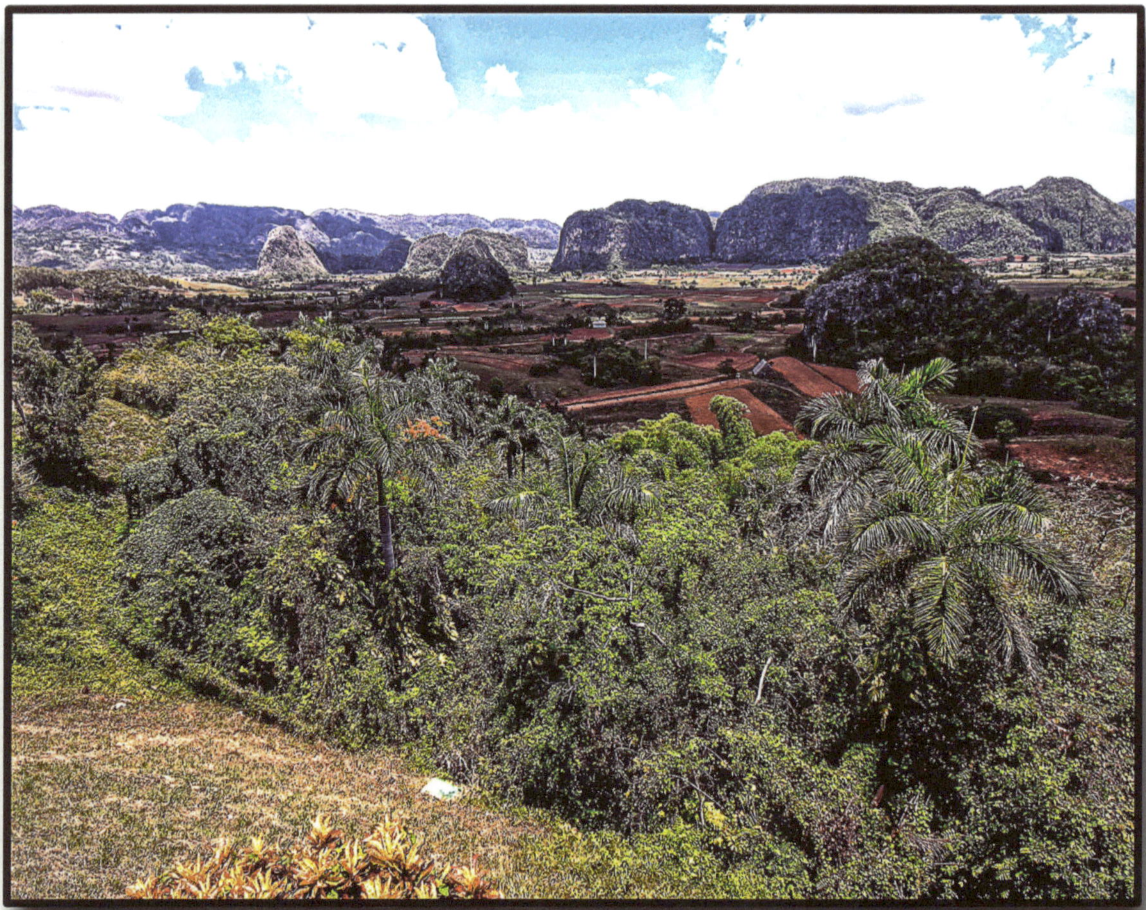

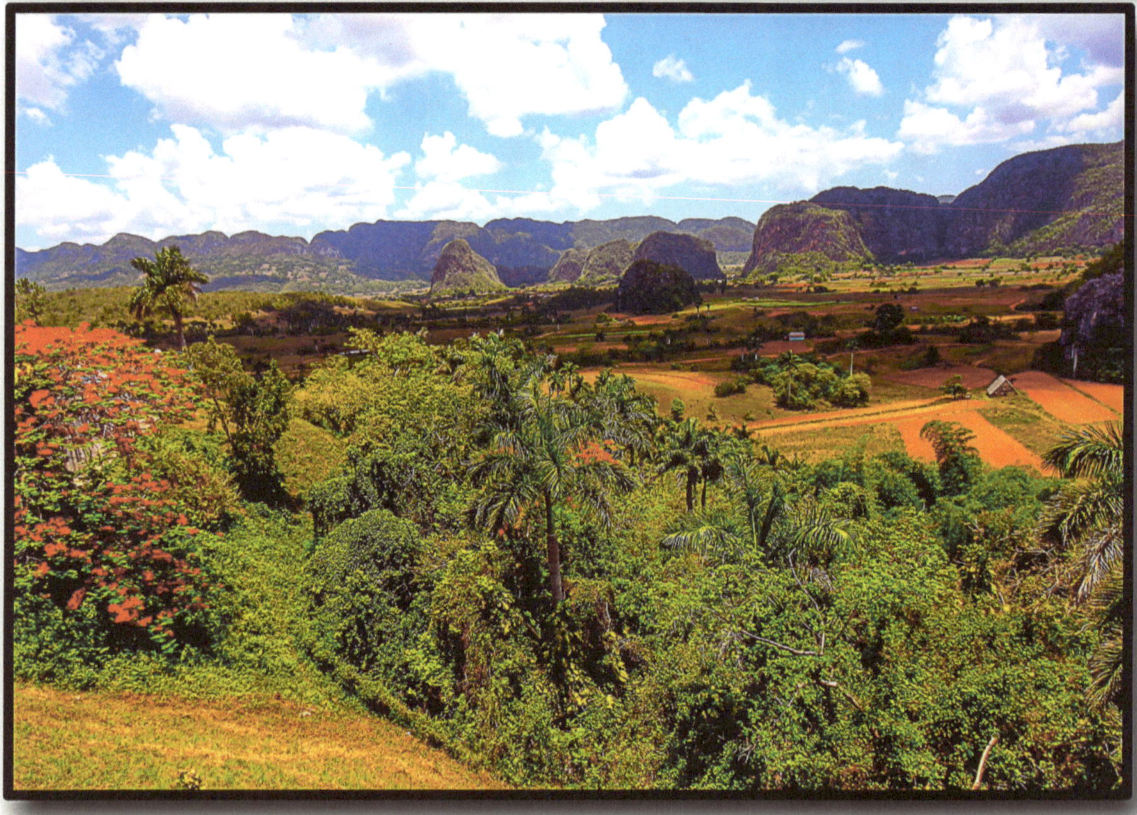

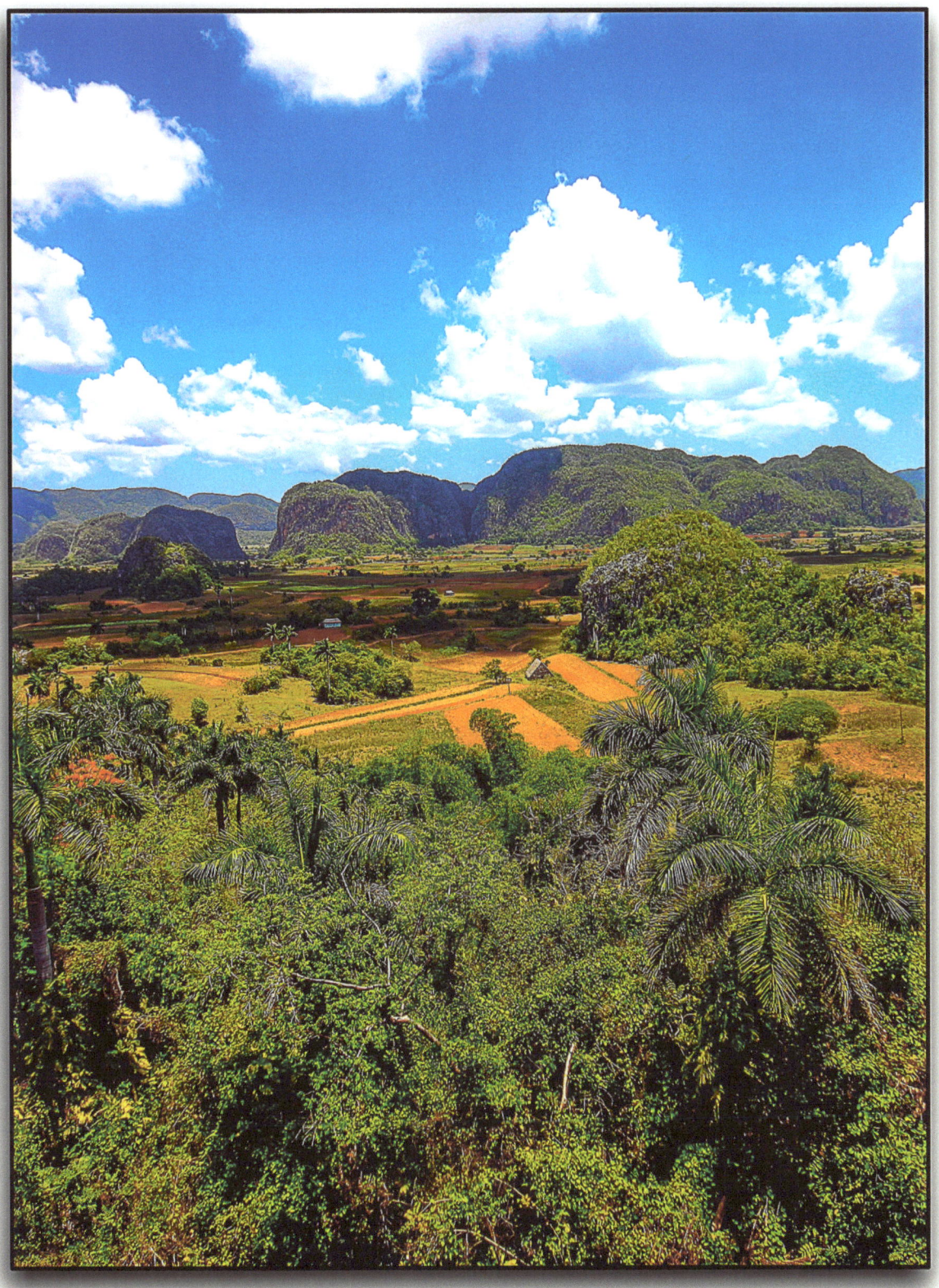

The preceding photos were taken from Los Jazmines, the highest view point in the whole Vinale valley overlooking the amazing and spectacular landscape. The Valley was named a World *Heritage* Site because of its natural beauty and the traditional agricultural techniques which continue to be used in the cultivation of some of Cuba's finest tobacco and other crops. Many of the mountainous hills in the backdown are dotted with indian caves.

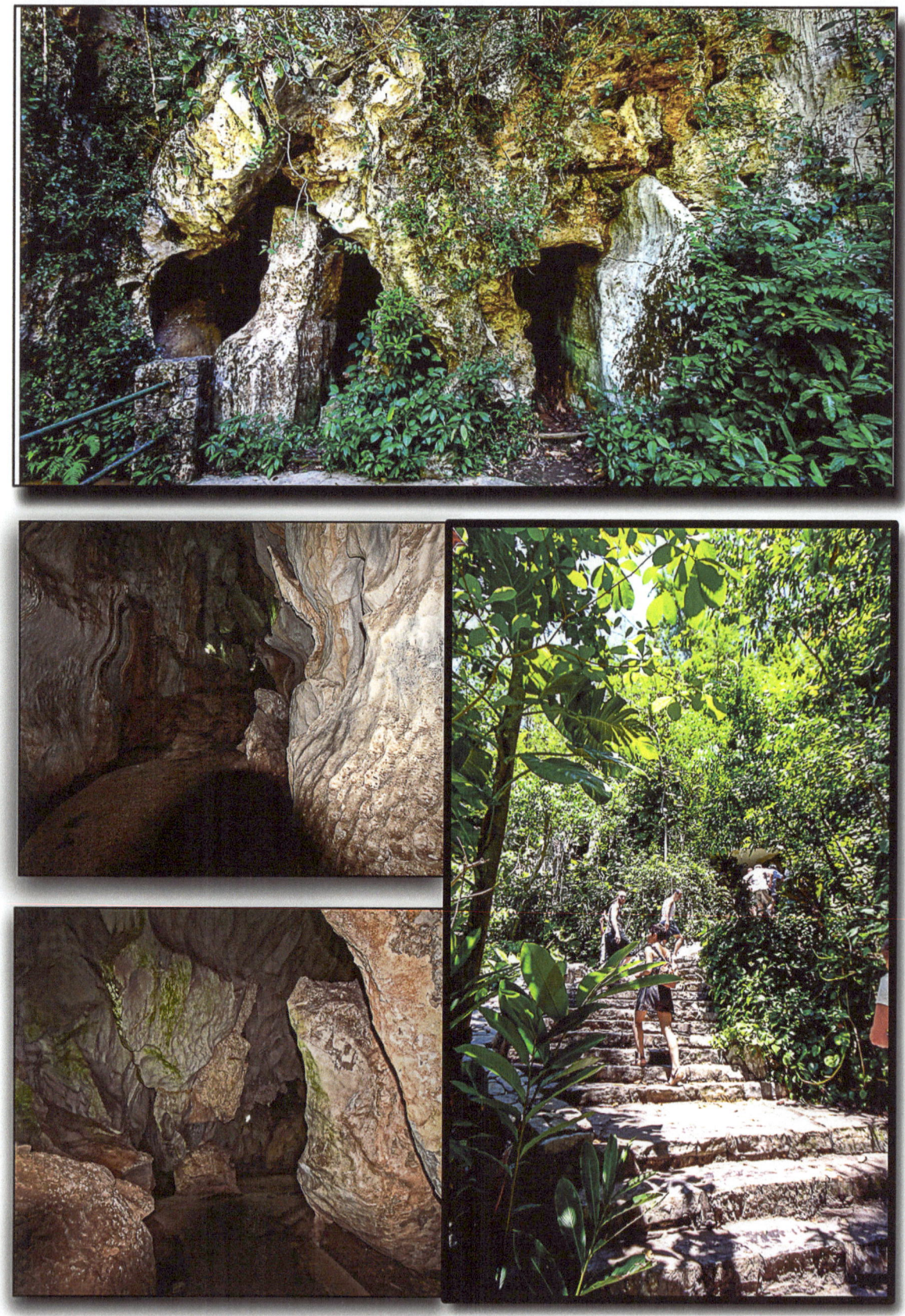

The Cuevas del Indio ("Indian Caves")

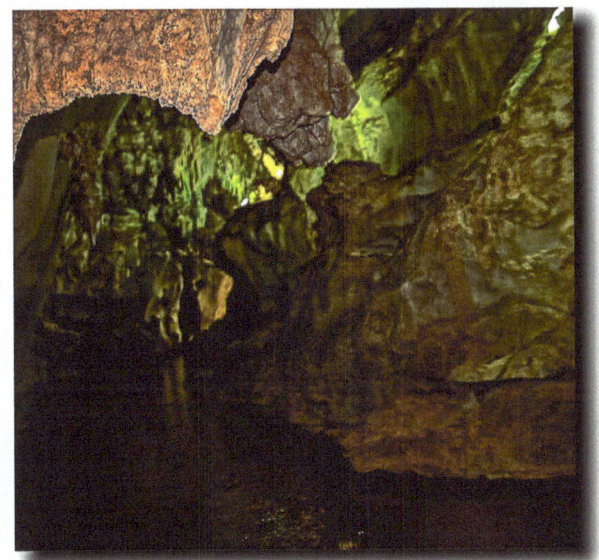
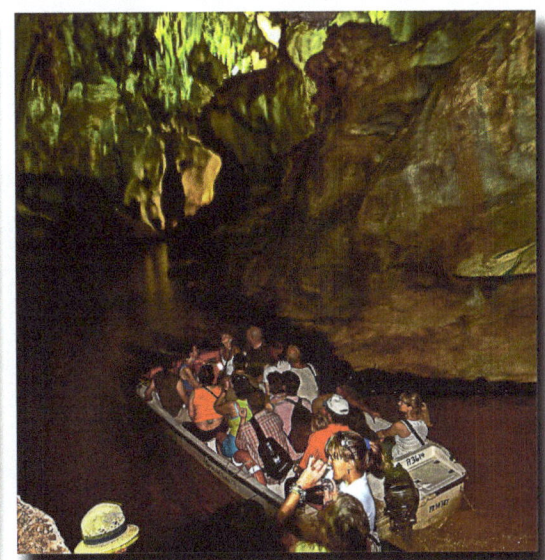
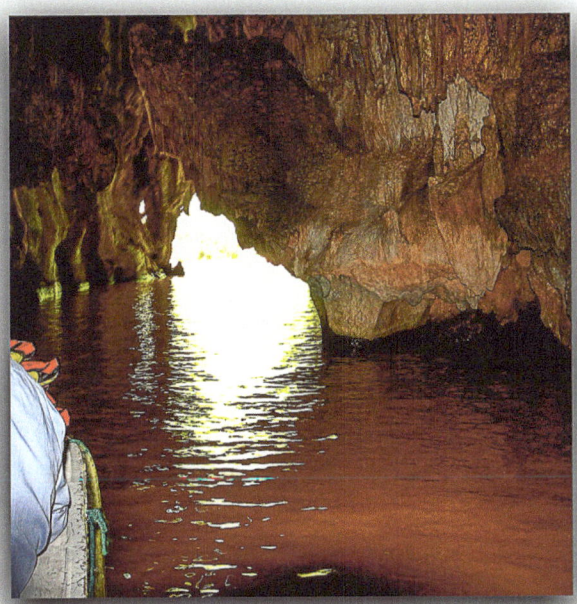
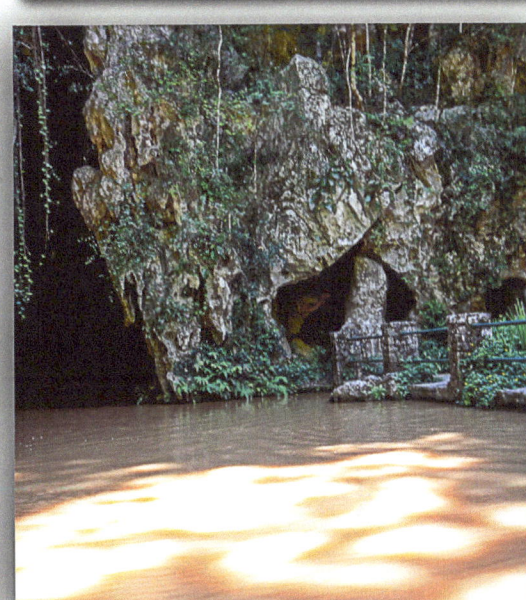
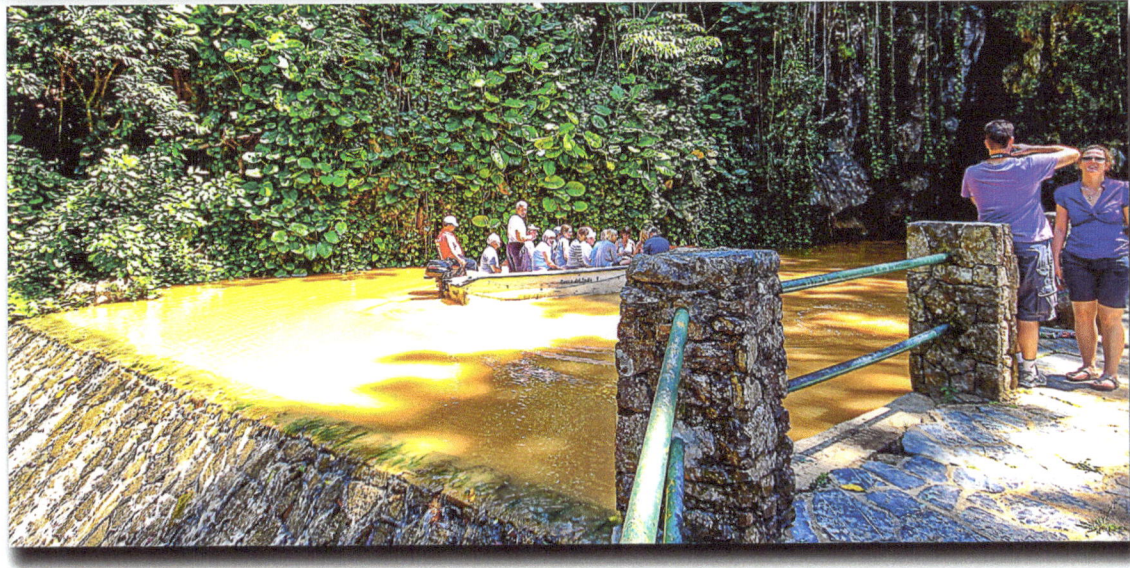

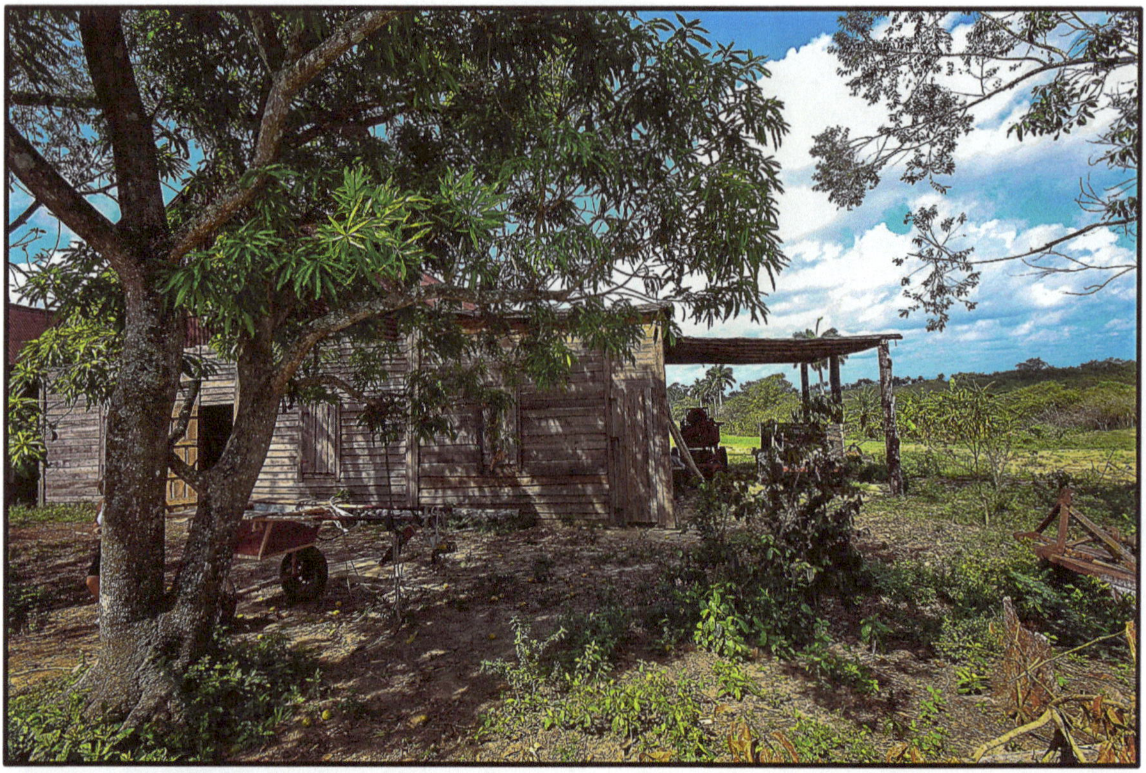

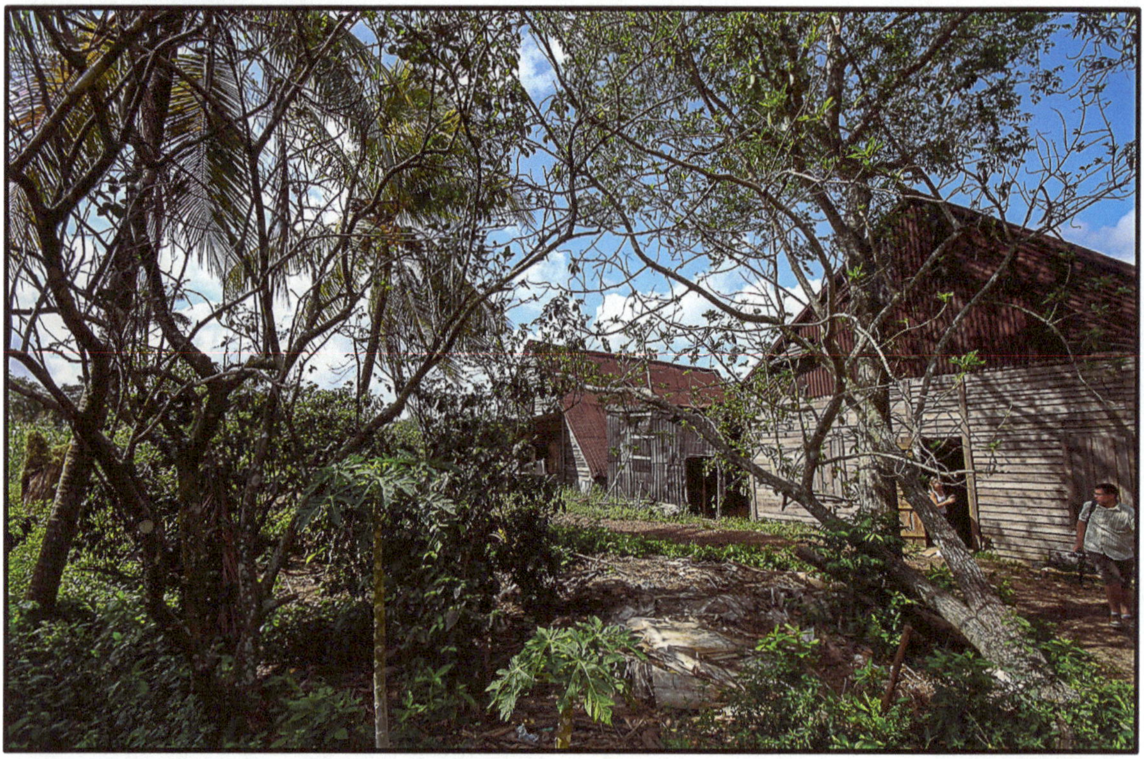

This is one of Cuba's over 30000 tobacco farms that produce some of the best tobacco leaves of the world that bring millions in profit to Cuba   There are 43 government controlled factories that process the tobacco.   As with any business in Cuba, 80% of profits go to the government. The tobacco leaves are cured and dried in these large barns and shipped to the factories.

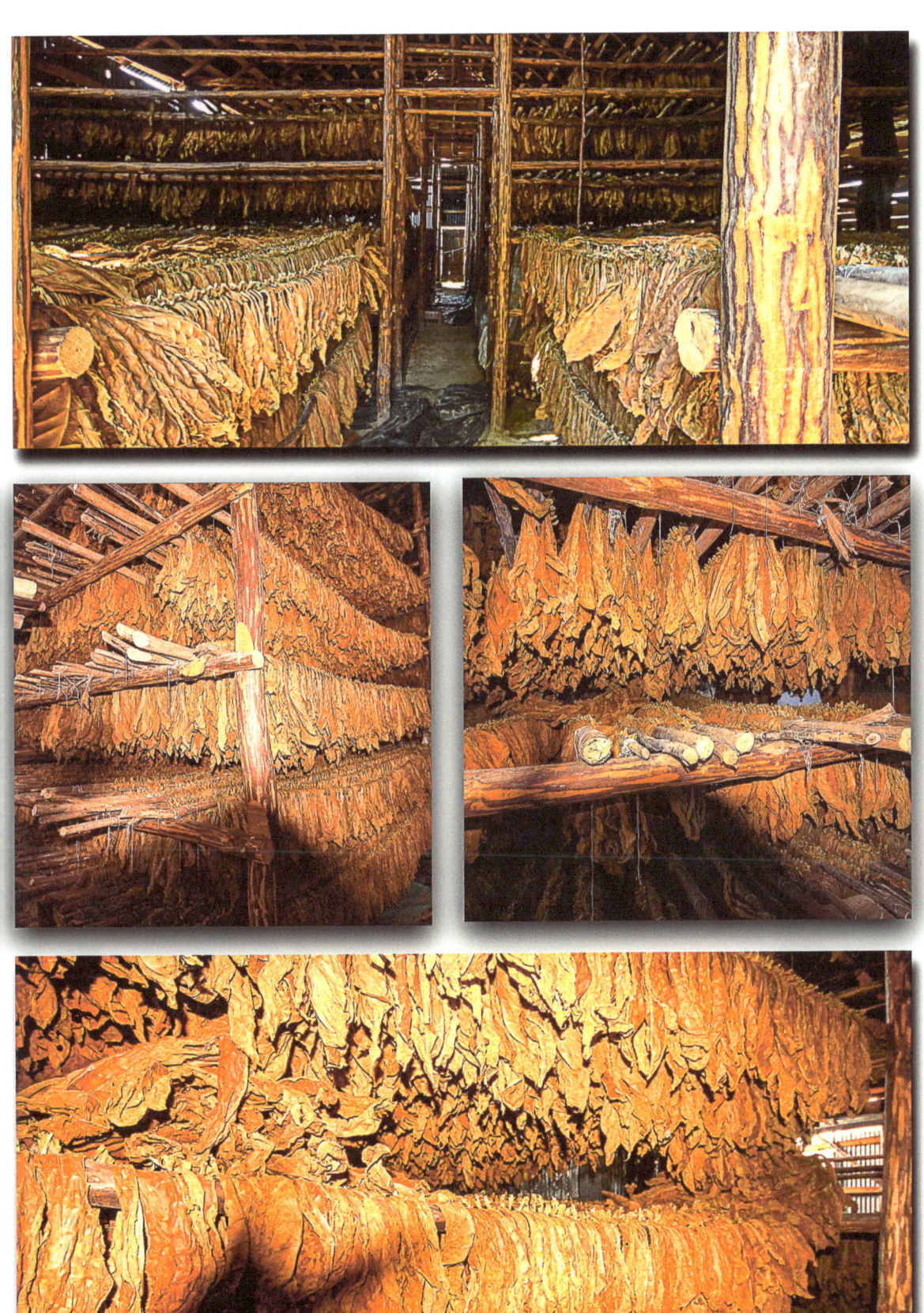

Inside the tobacco barns where the leaves are cured and dried.

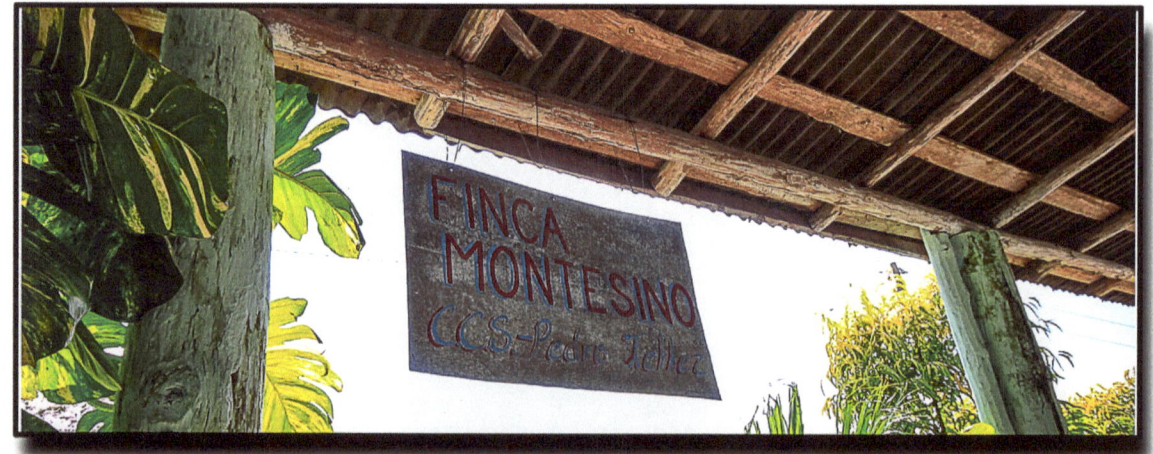

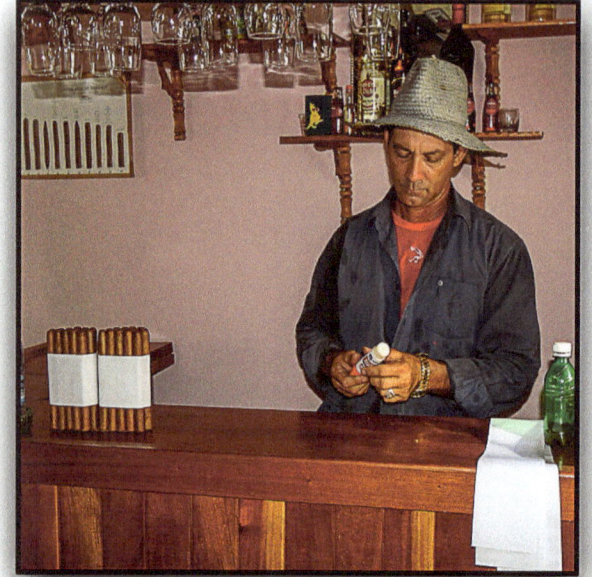

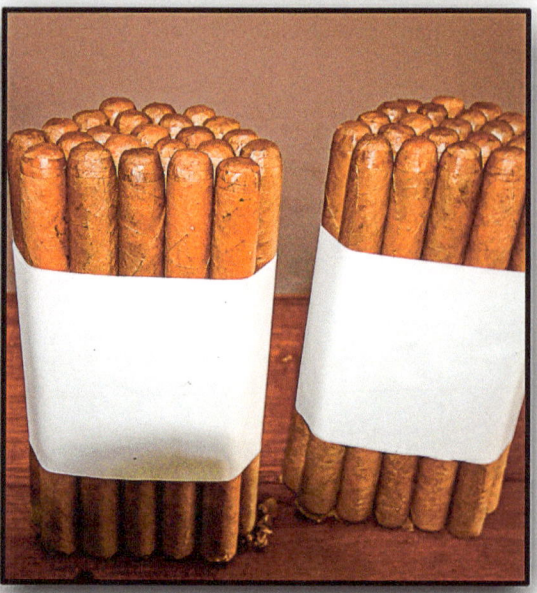

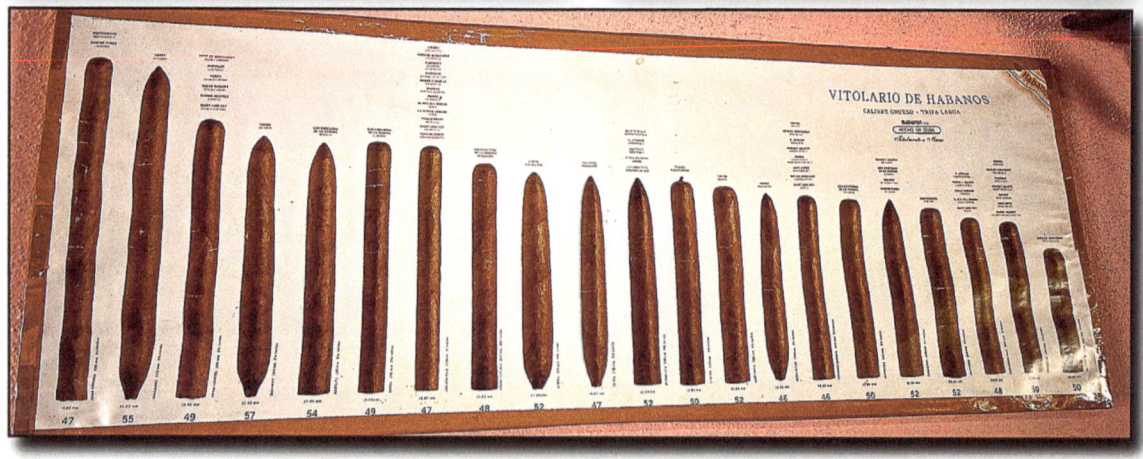

The Cuban Cigar comes in many quality grades and many sizes depending of what part of the tobacco leaf it is cut from. The most expensive is cut and hand rolled from the heart of the leaf and the least expensive is mechine rolled from the leftover scraps of the leaf. No parts of the leaf is discarded. Though most of the tobacco leaves go to the government controlled factories for processing, the farmers are allow to keep some for private use and get a chance to sell some products illegally to tourist in order to keep more of their profits.

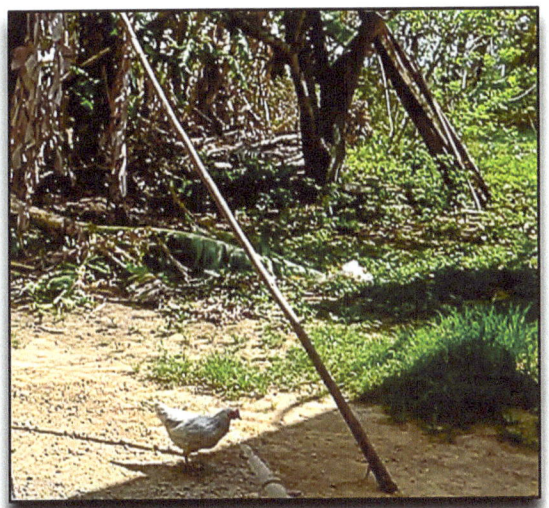
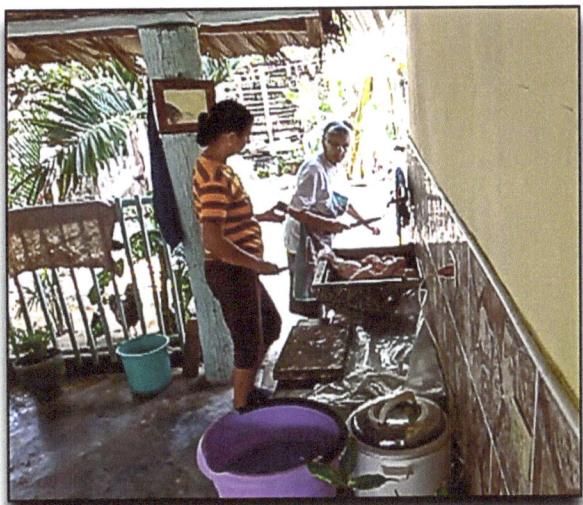
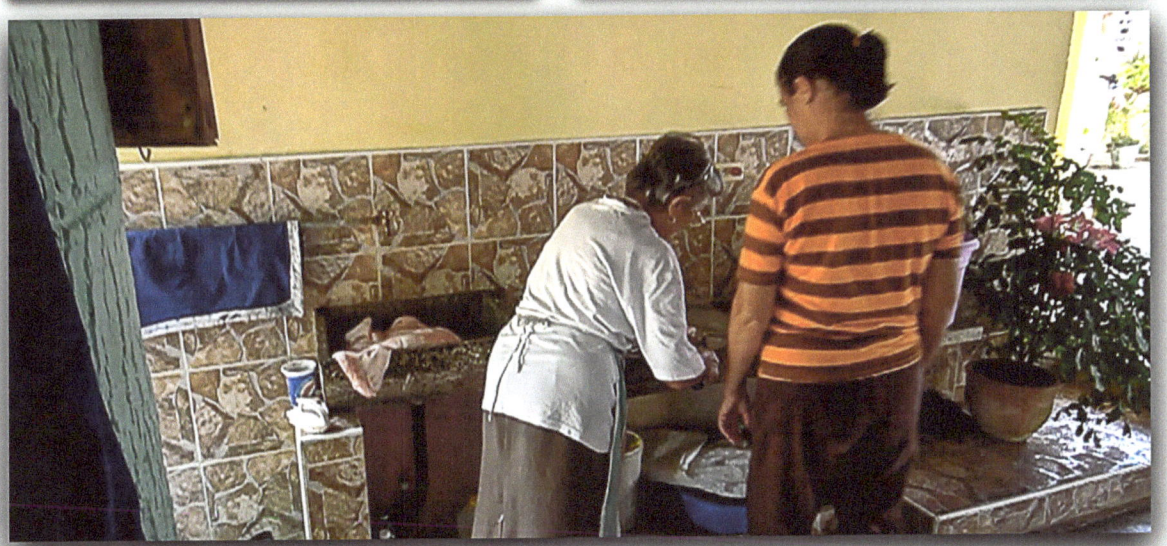
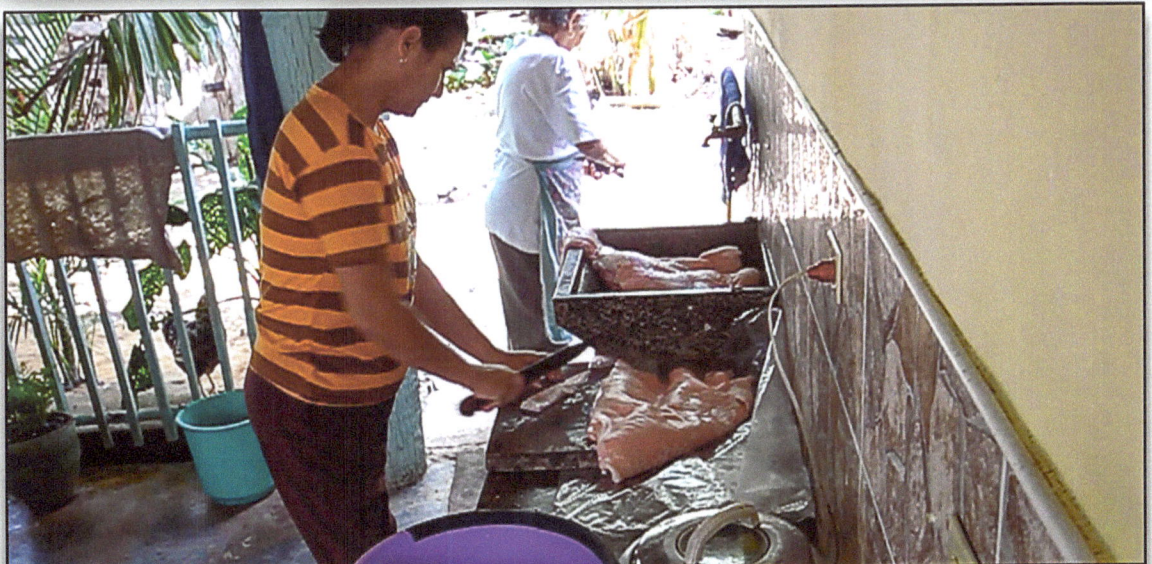

Farmers raise and slaughter there own small animals, such as pigs and chickens. Here Grandma passes on the trade of meat preparation . She demonstrates how to sharpen the knife, clean the meat, and make the surgical cuts of a skillful butcher. The daughter learns well.

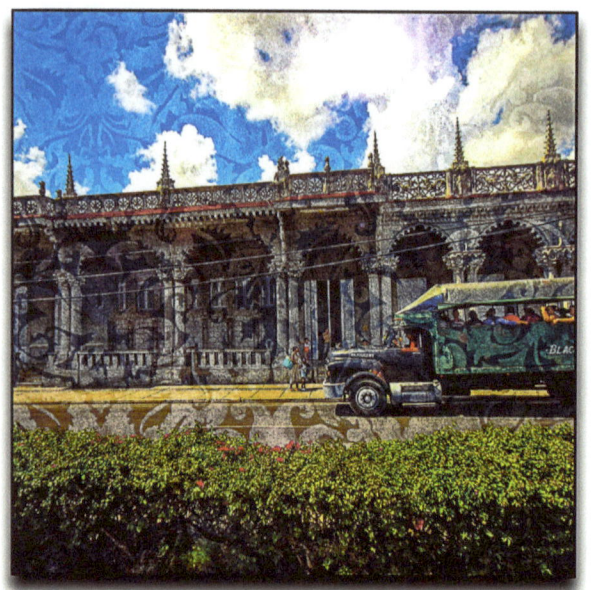
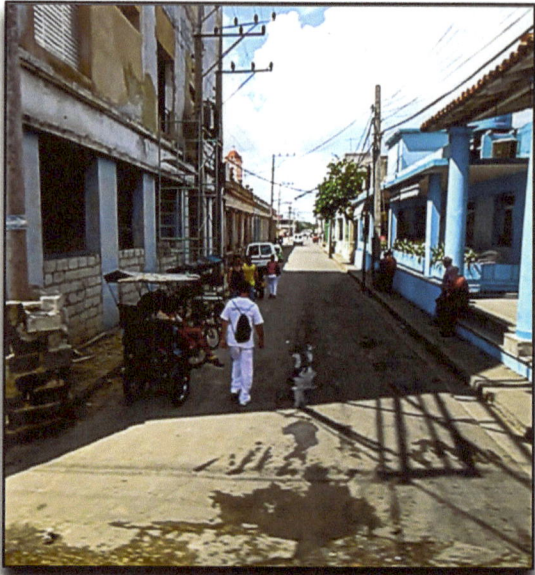
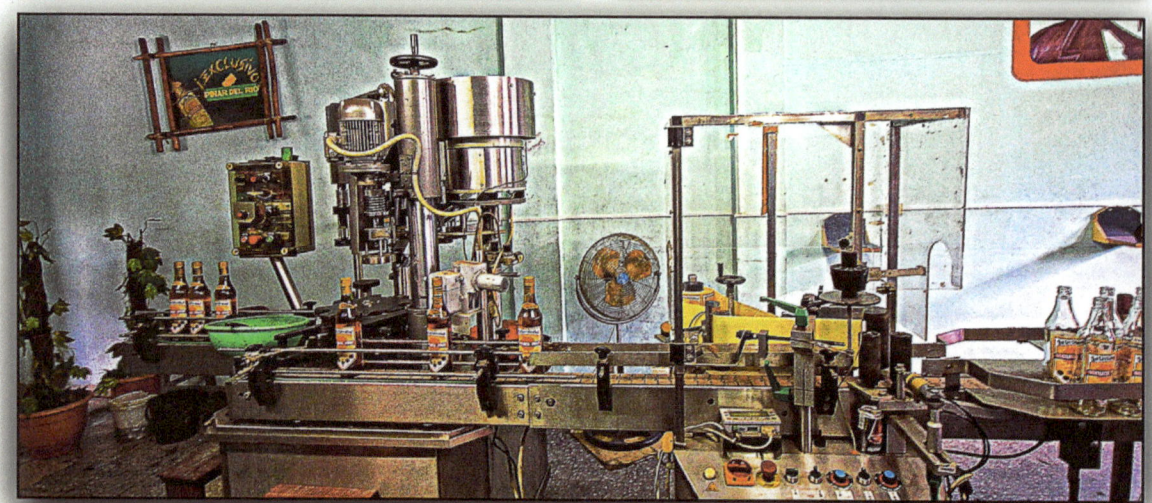
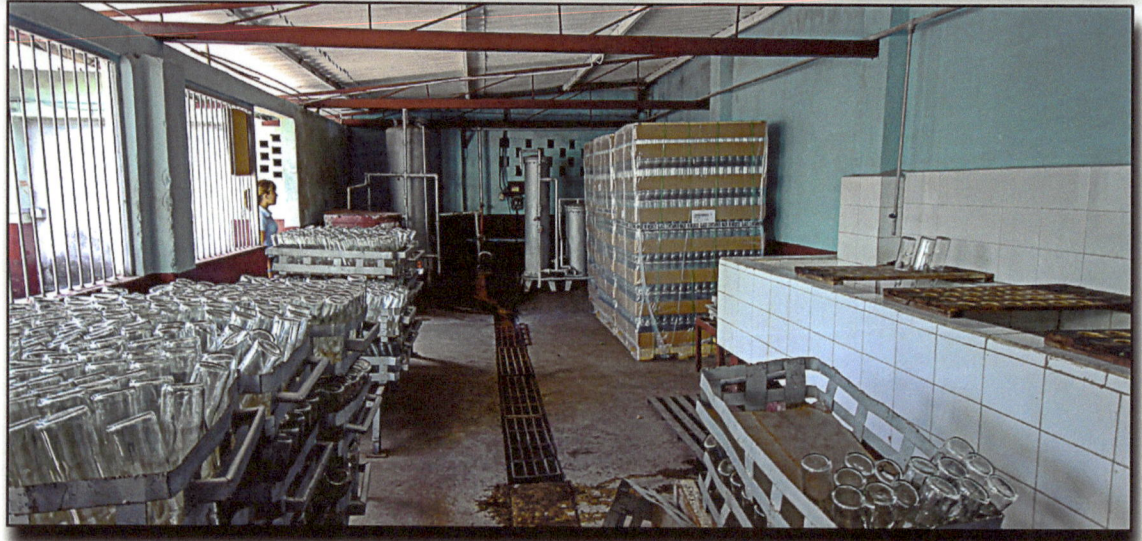

Cuba is known throughout the world for its cigars and rum. This is a rum bottling factoy in the city of vinales.

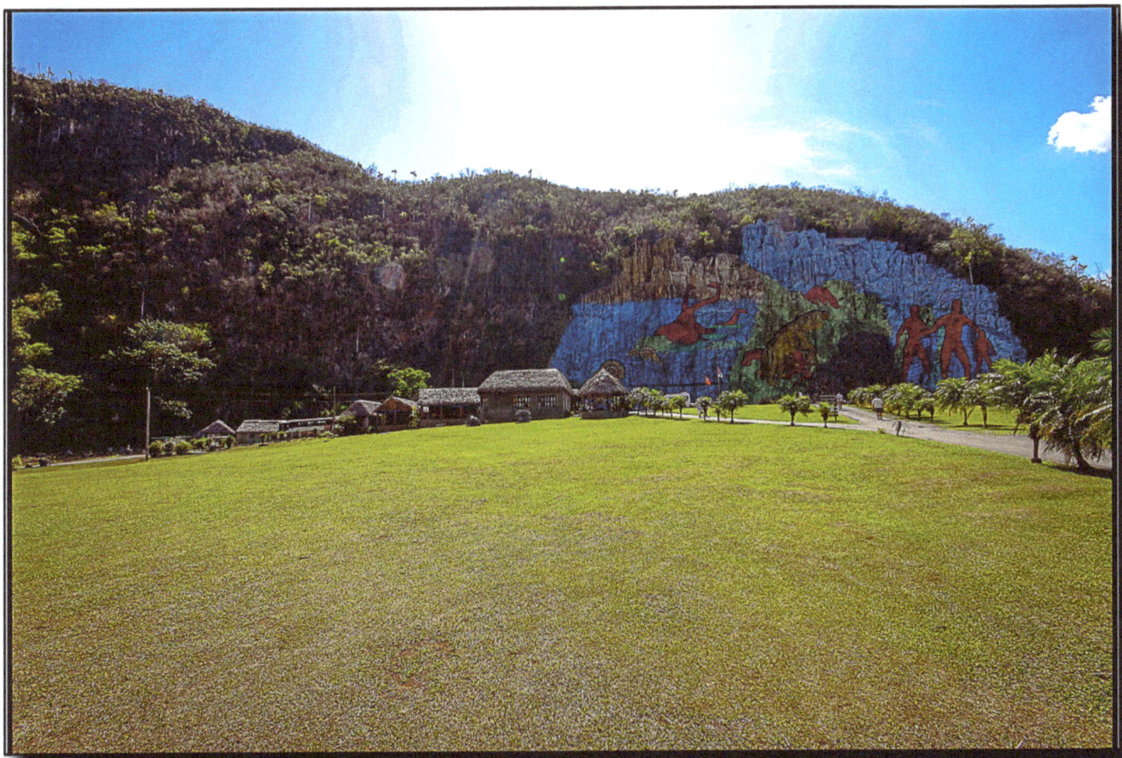

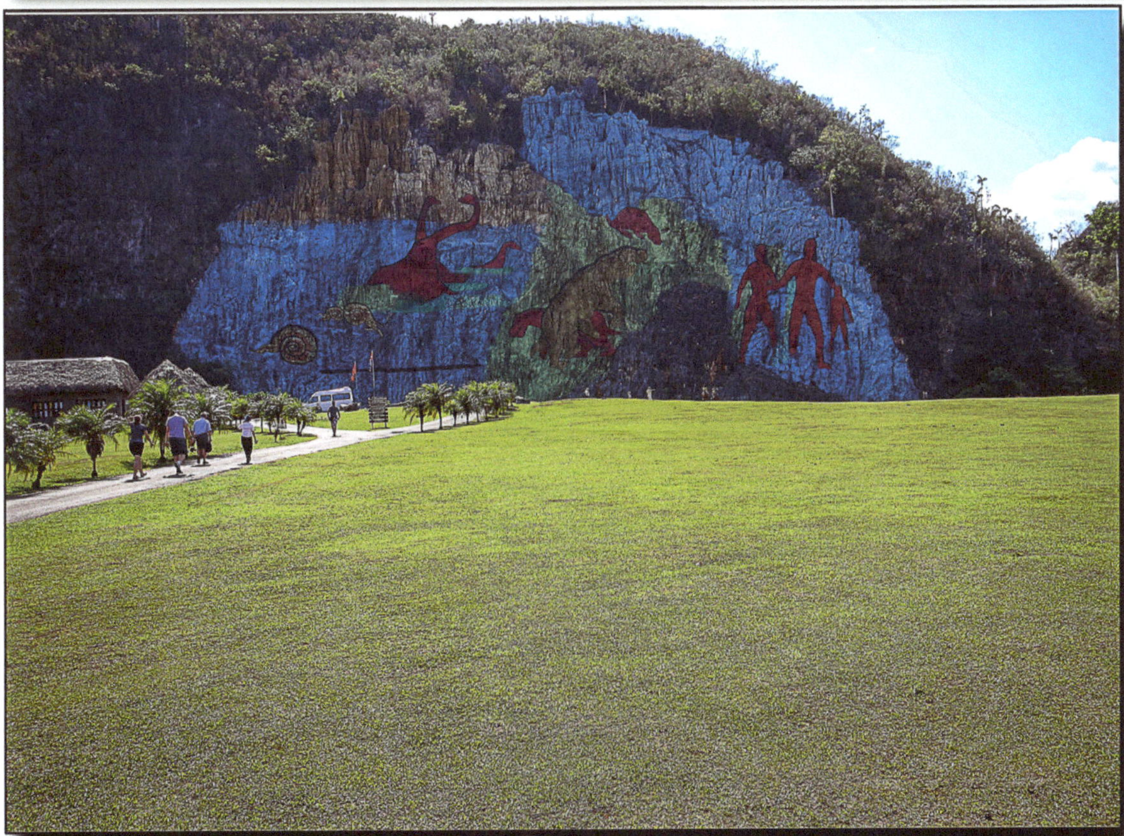

Mural de la Prehistoria: In 1961 Fidel Castro visited a beautiful valley situated a short distance west of Vinales. He commissioned that the cliff should be painted with dinosaurs and a family of cave people.

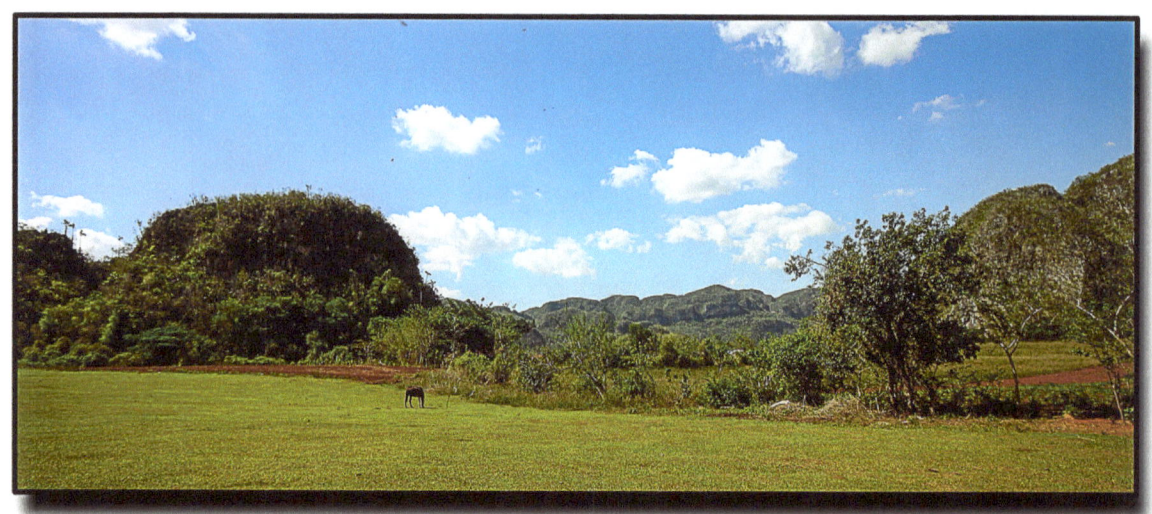

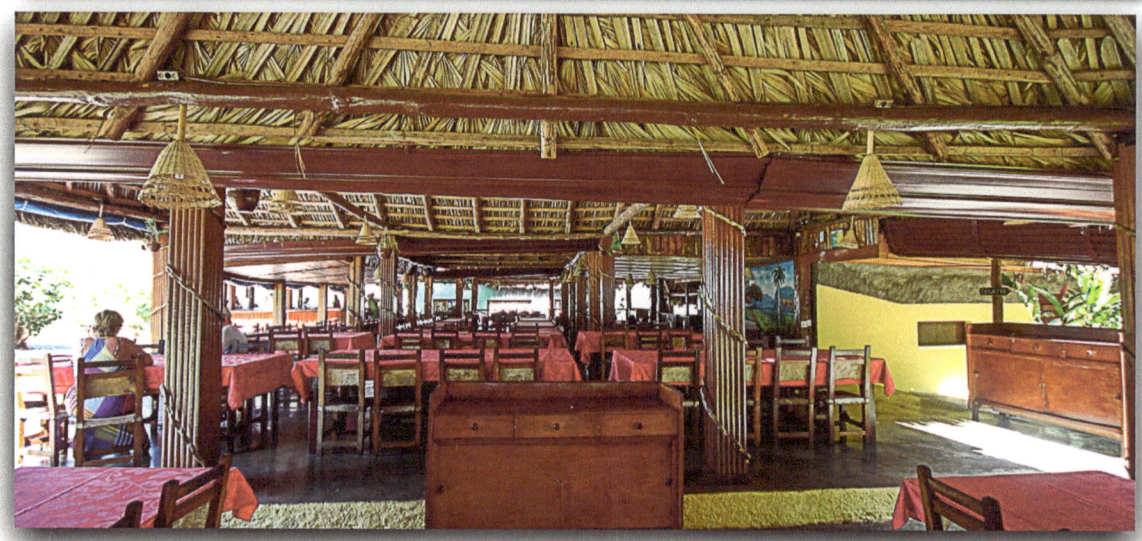

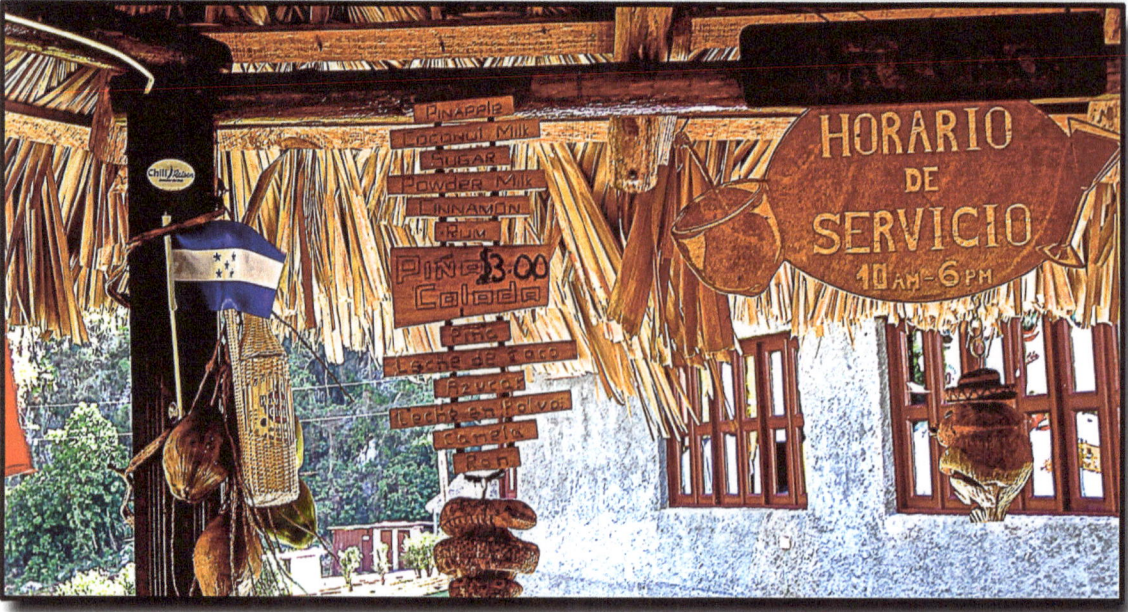

This little cafe bar on the grounds of Mural de la Prehistoria has the most delicious, mouth watering Pina Colada you could ever dream of tasting…and, they share the recipe.

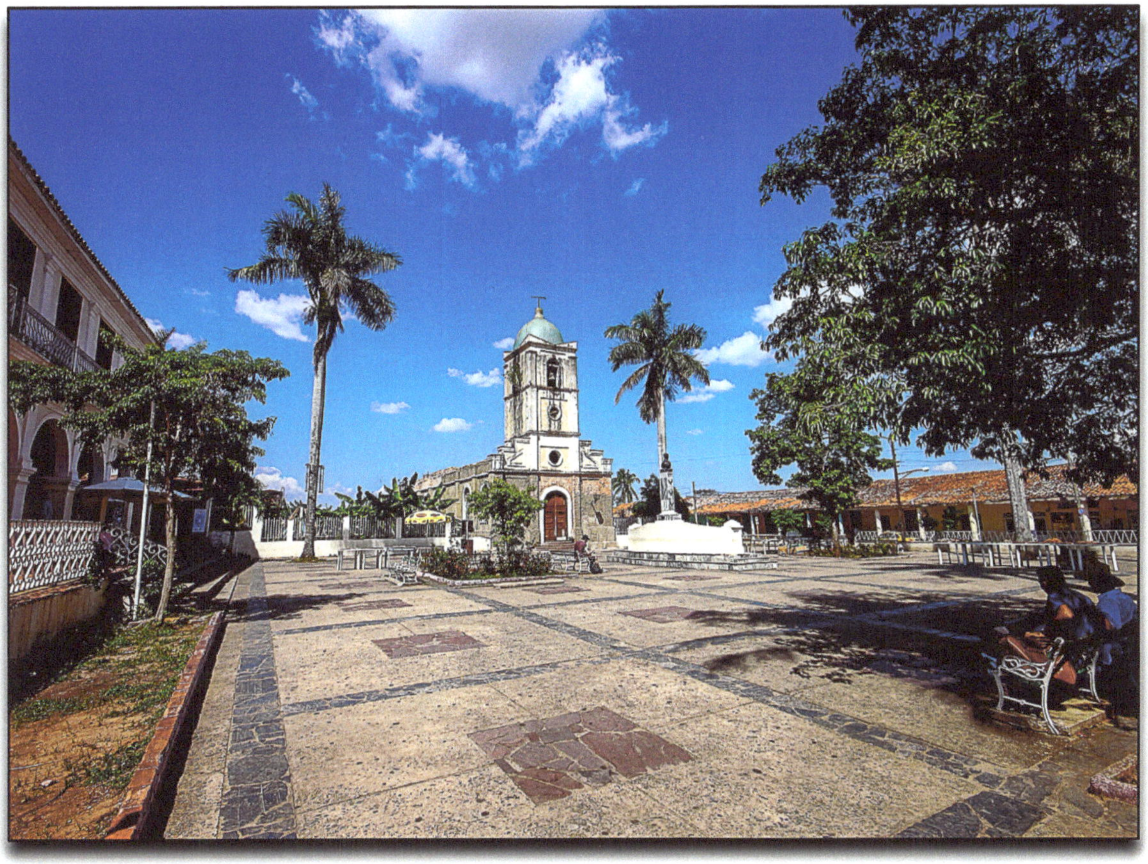

The church of the Cuban town of Vinales in the Pinar Del Rio province

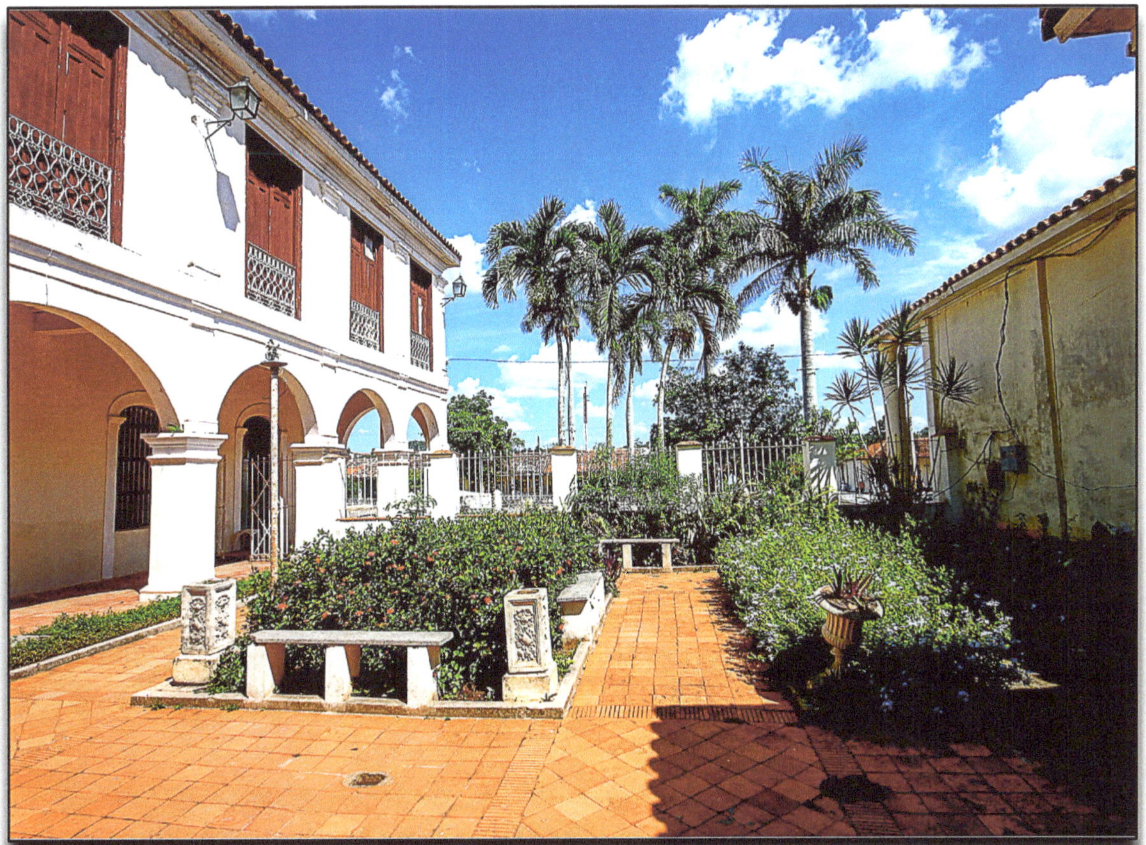

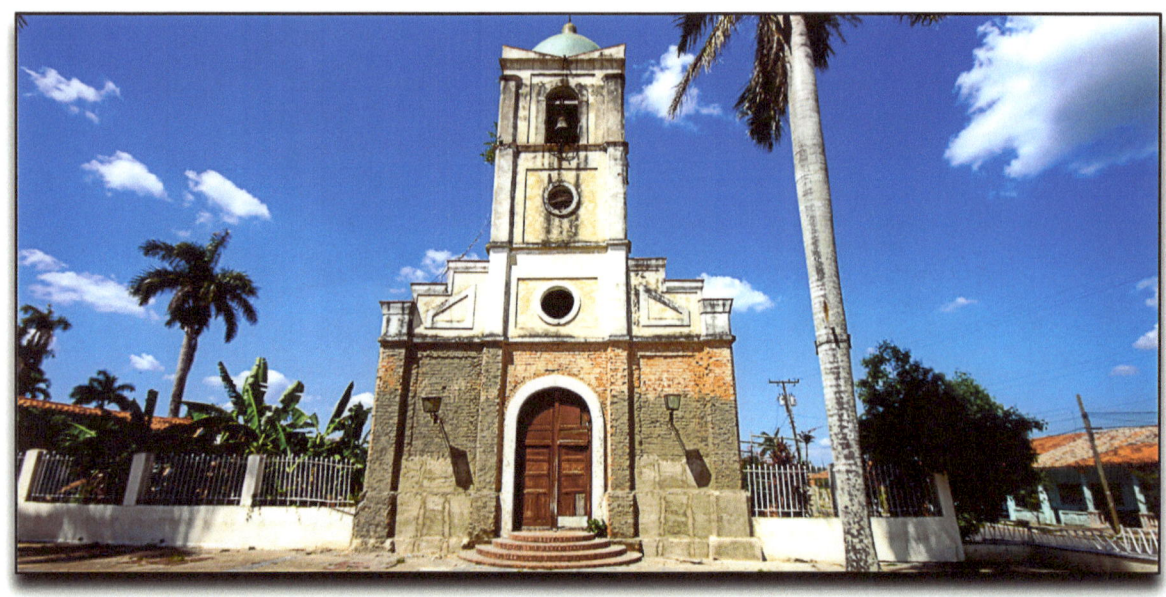

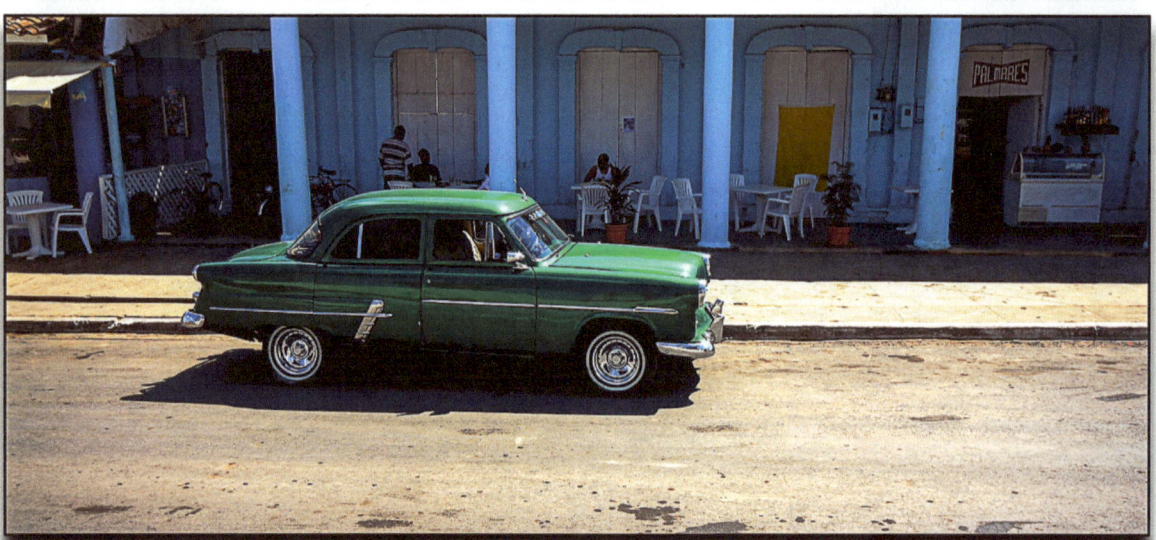

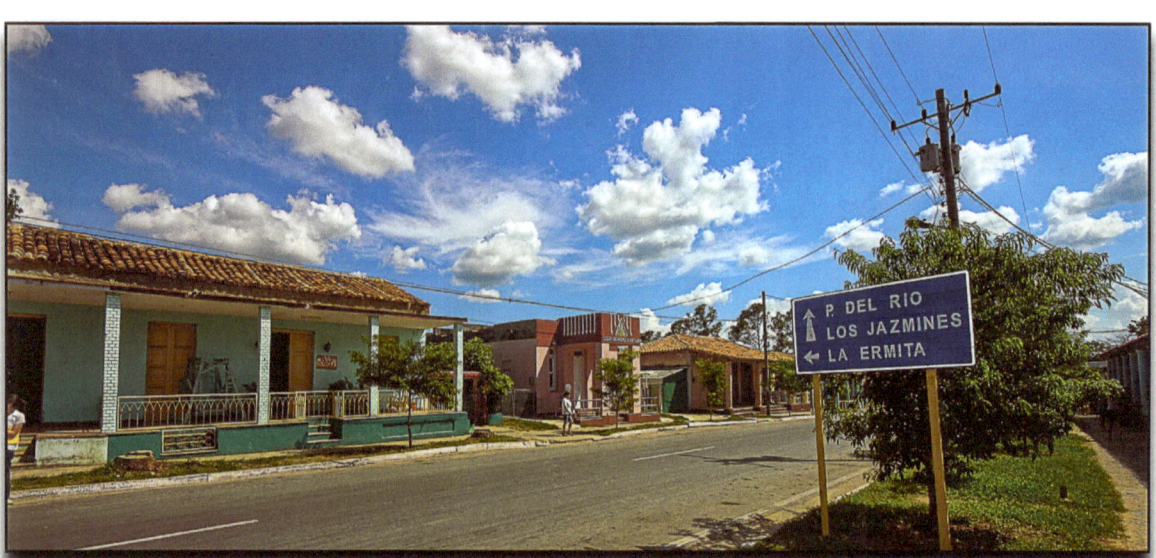

Leaving the beautiful Vinales Valley

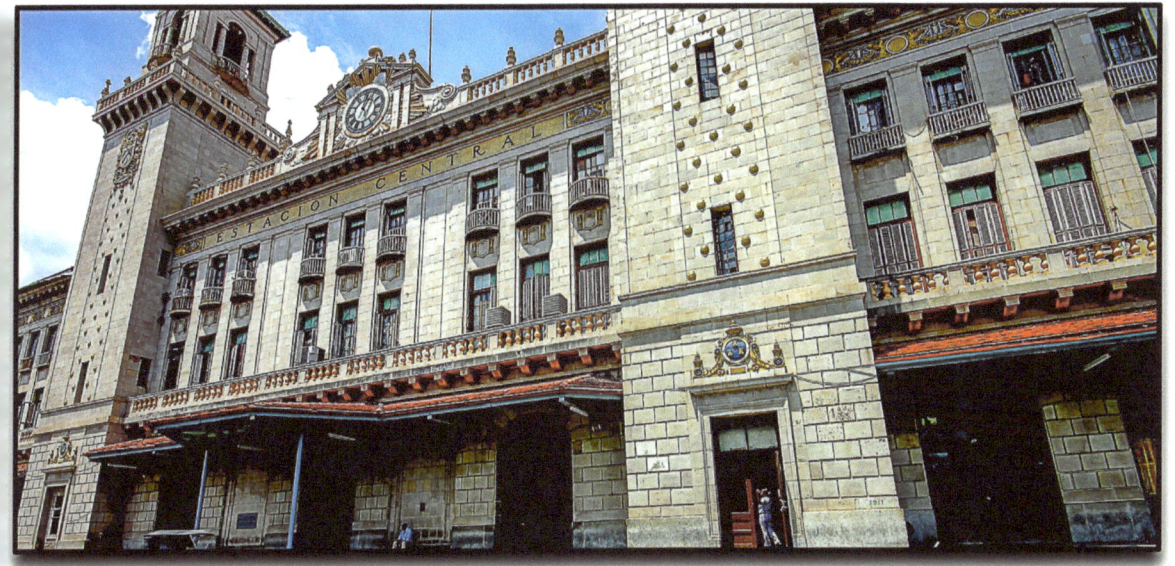

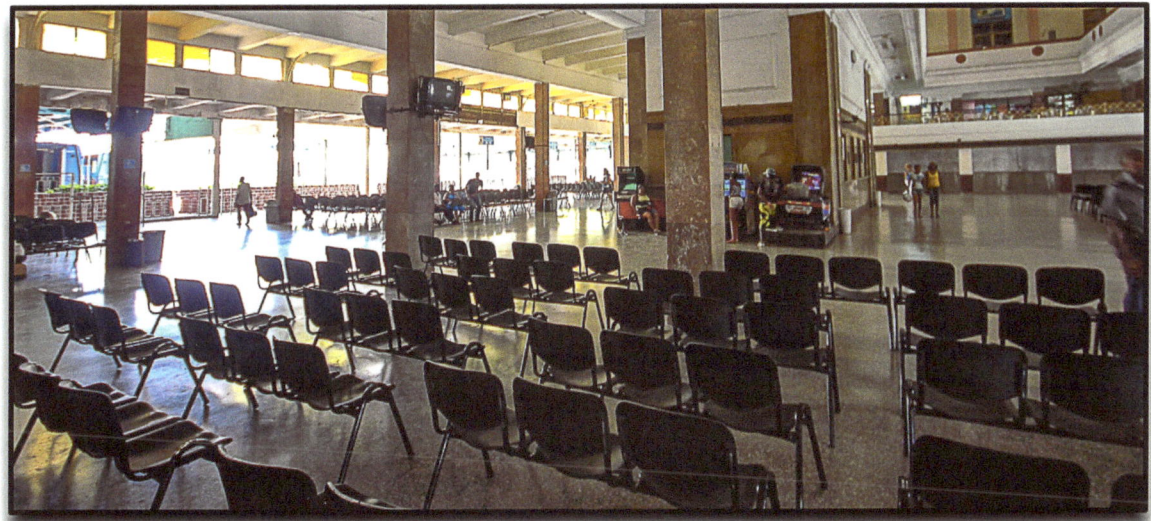

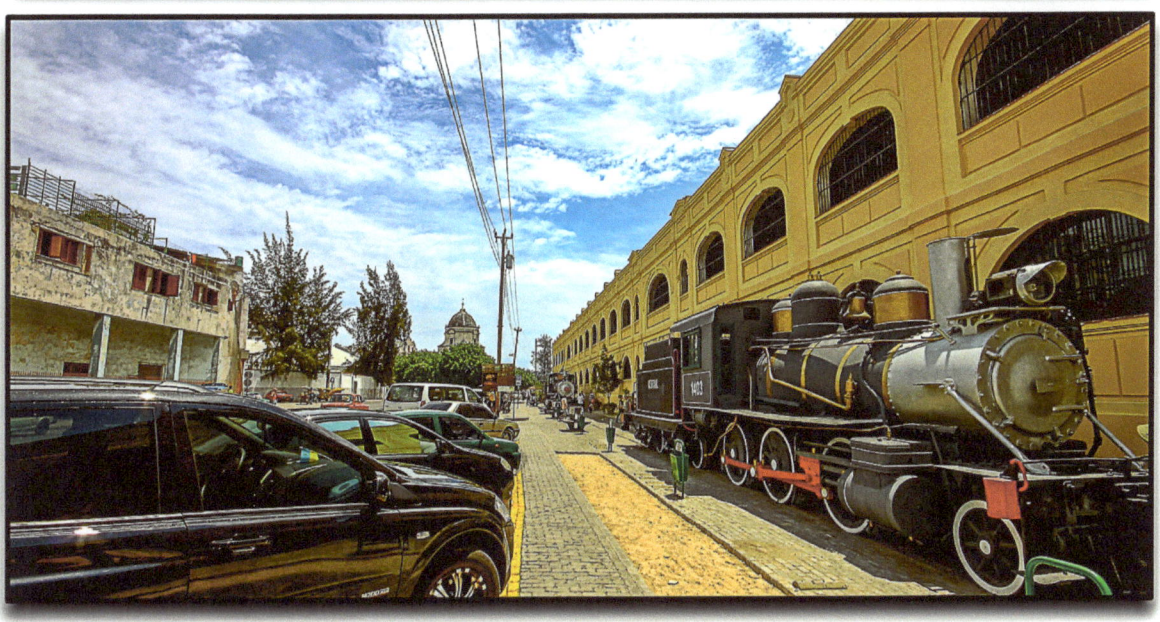

Havana Central railway station

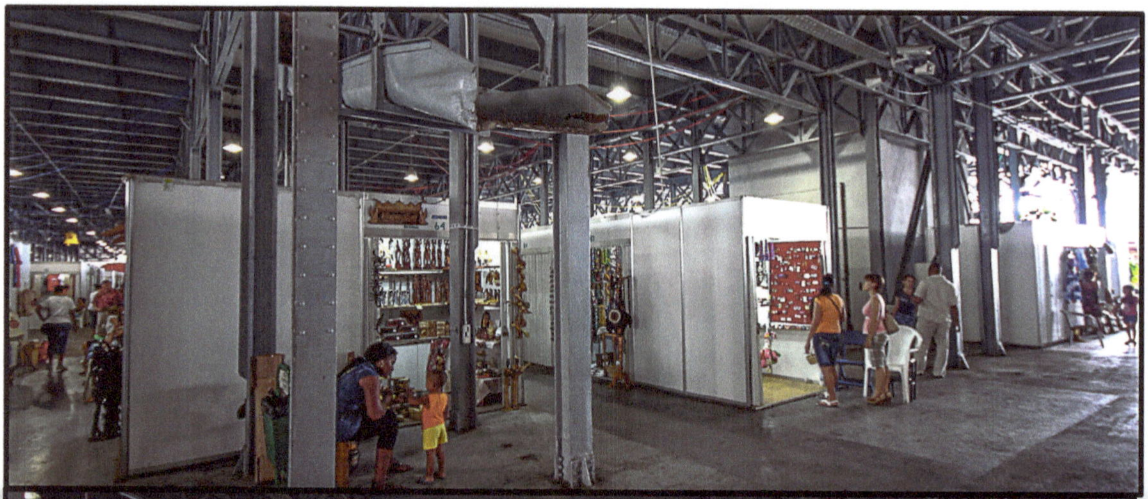

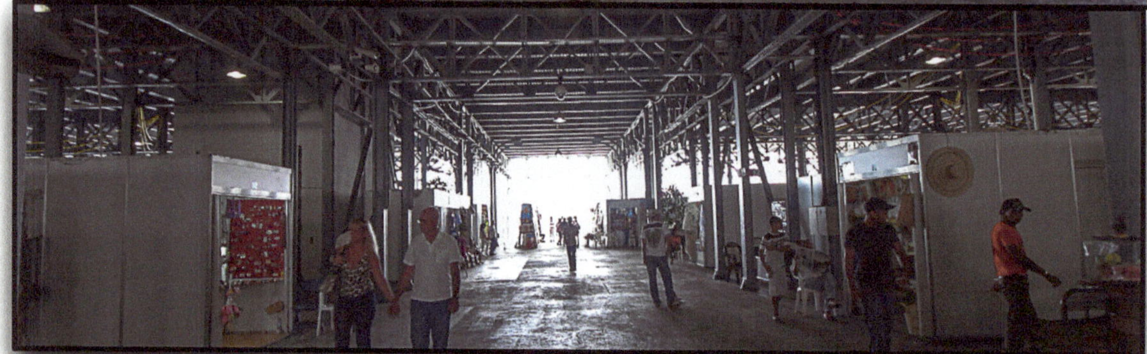

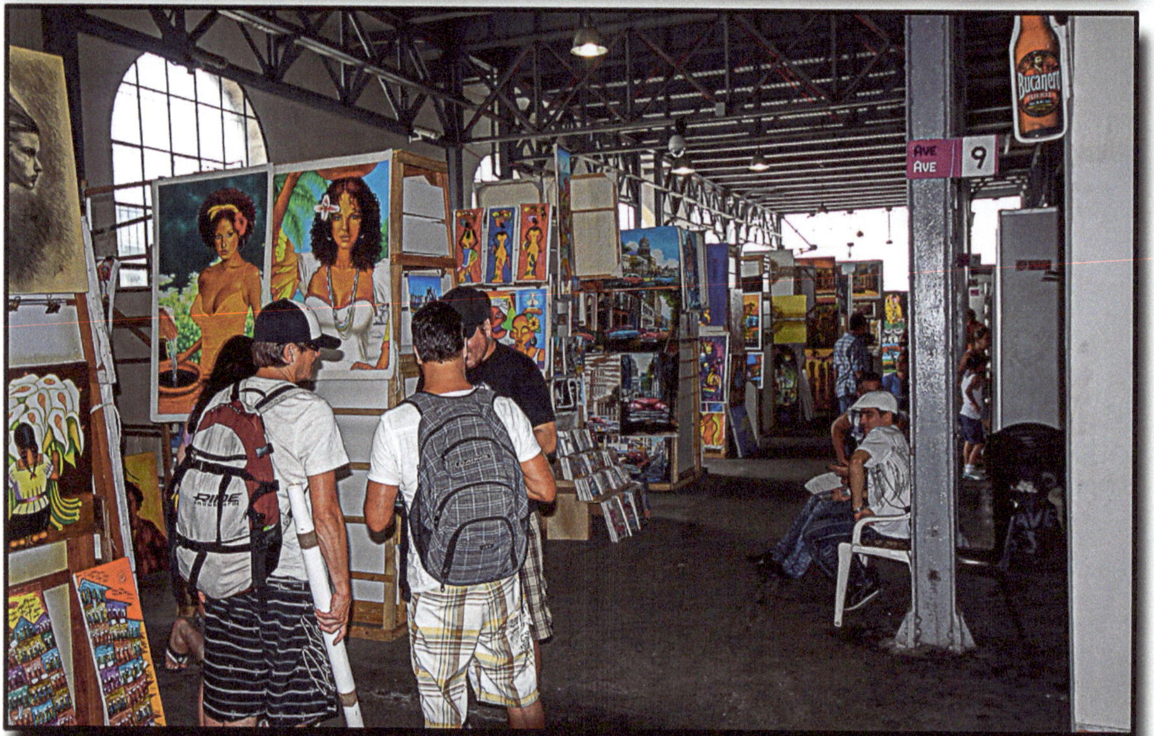

Havana's Craft and Souvenir Market, now located alongside the inner harbour on Desampardos, is an old warehouse-like structure filled with individual stalls that offer artwork and crafts, as well as souvenirs typical to cuban obsessions such as cigar boxes, domino sets, baseball paraphernalia and Havana Club-branded trinkets. Cuban art must have a documentation stamp in oder to go through customs. No stamp, it will be confiscated.

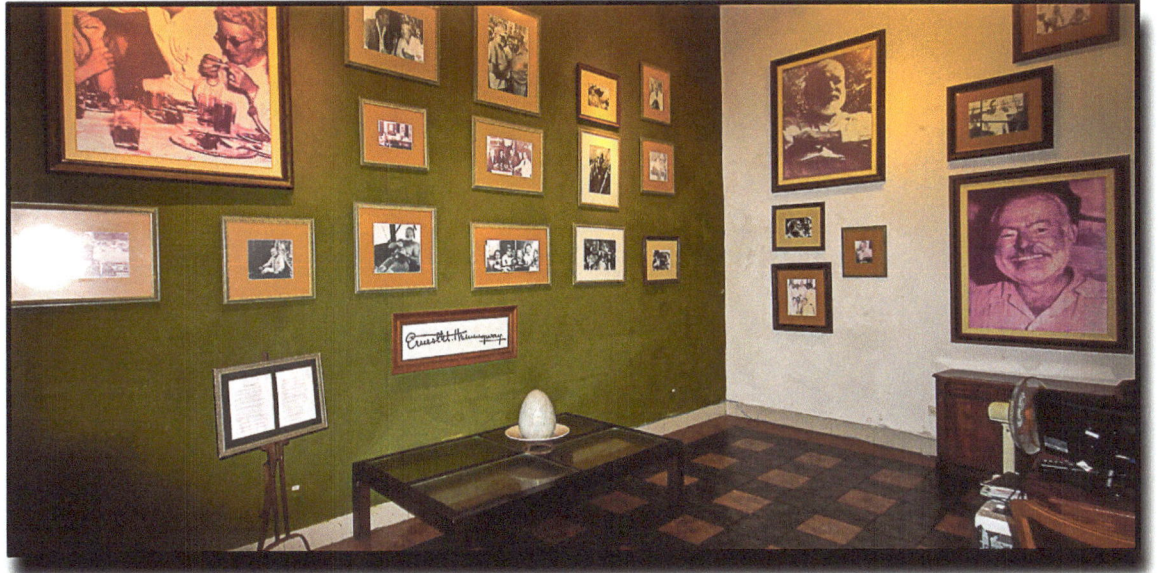

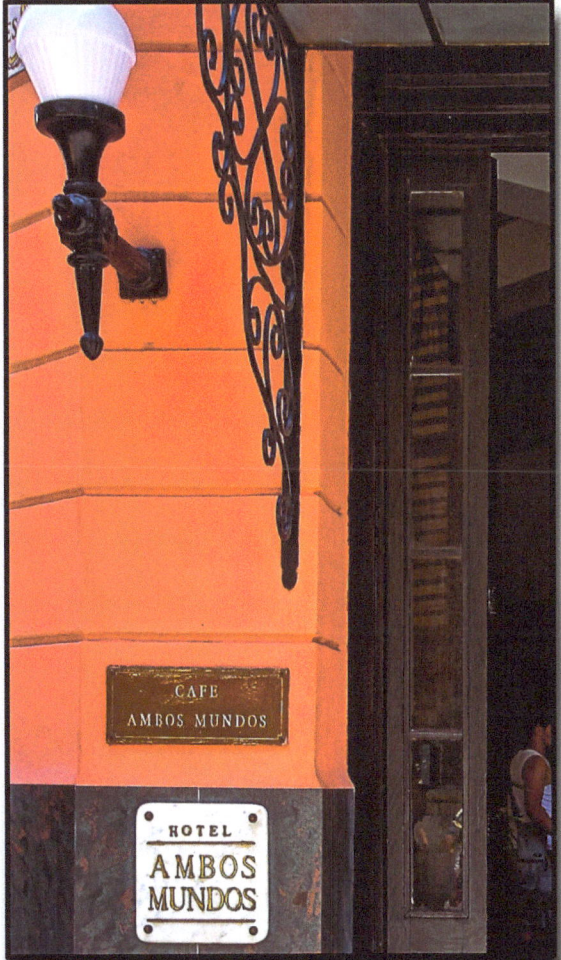

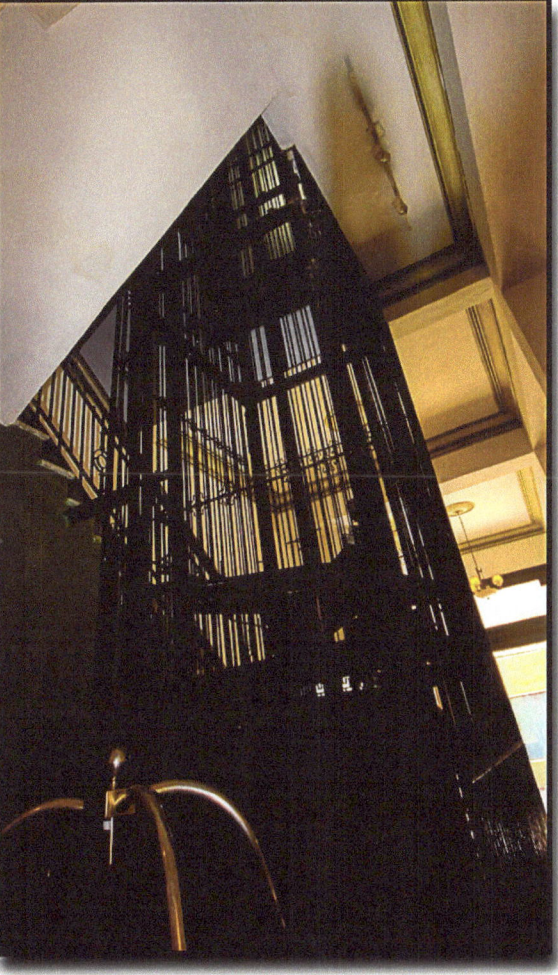

In1932, room 515 on the upper 5th floor in The Ambos Mundos Hotel became the "first home" in Cuba of writer Ernest Hemingway. Here he enjoyed the views of Old Havana, and the harbor sea in which he often fished. He occupied the room until mid-1939 prior to moving his winter home to Key West Flordia. Today that room is preserved as a museum, and the corner of the ground floor hotel lobby has two walls of framed photographs dedicated to the famous writer.

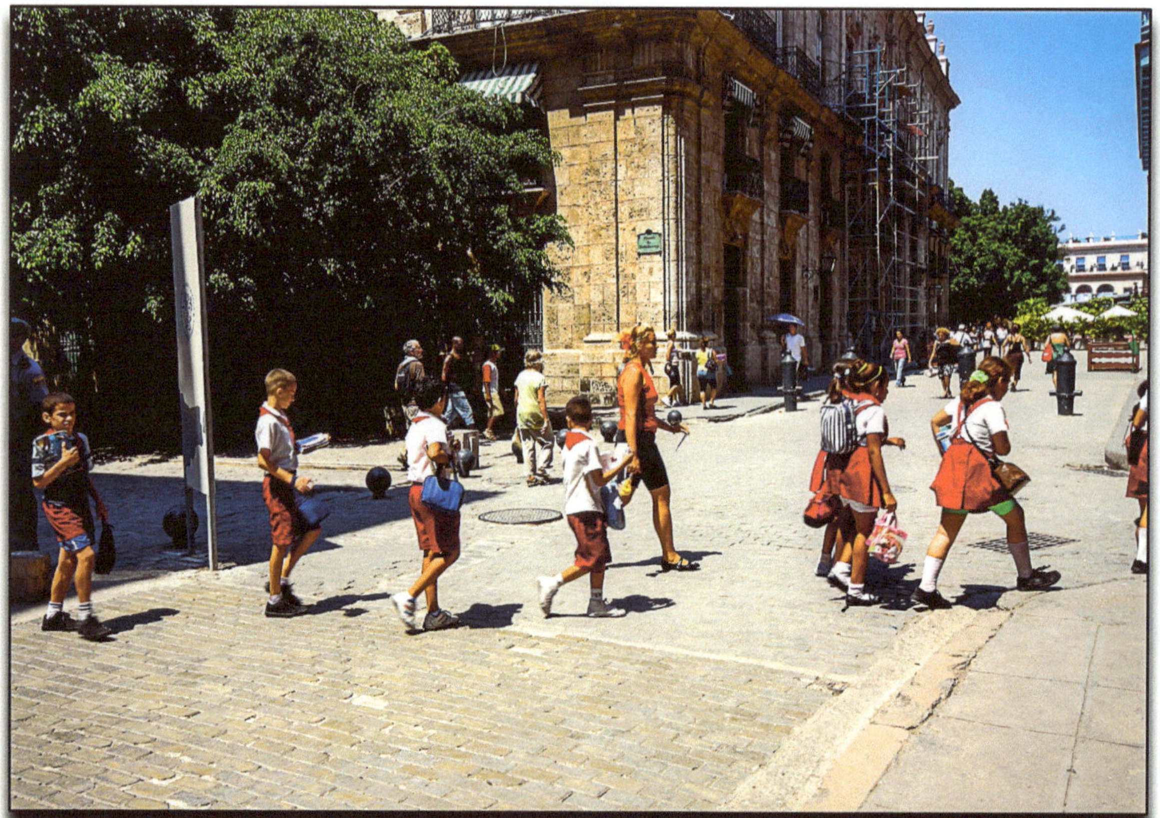

Health and education is governed owned and run and is a basic right in Cuba and free at all levels. School attendance is compulsory to the end of age 15. Children all ages regardless of gender must wear school uniforms with the color denoting their grade levels. Cuba's literacy rate is 99.8 percent.

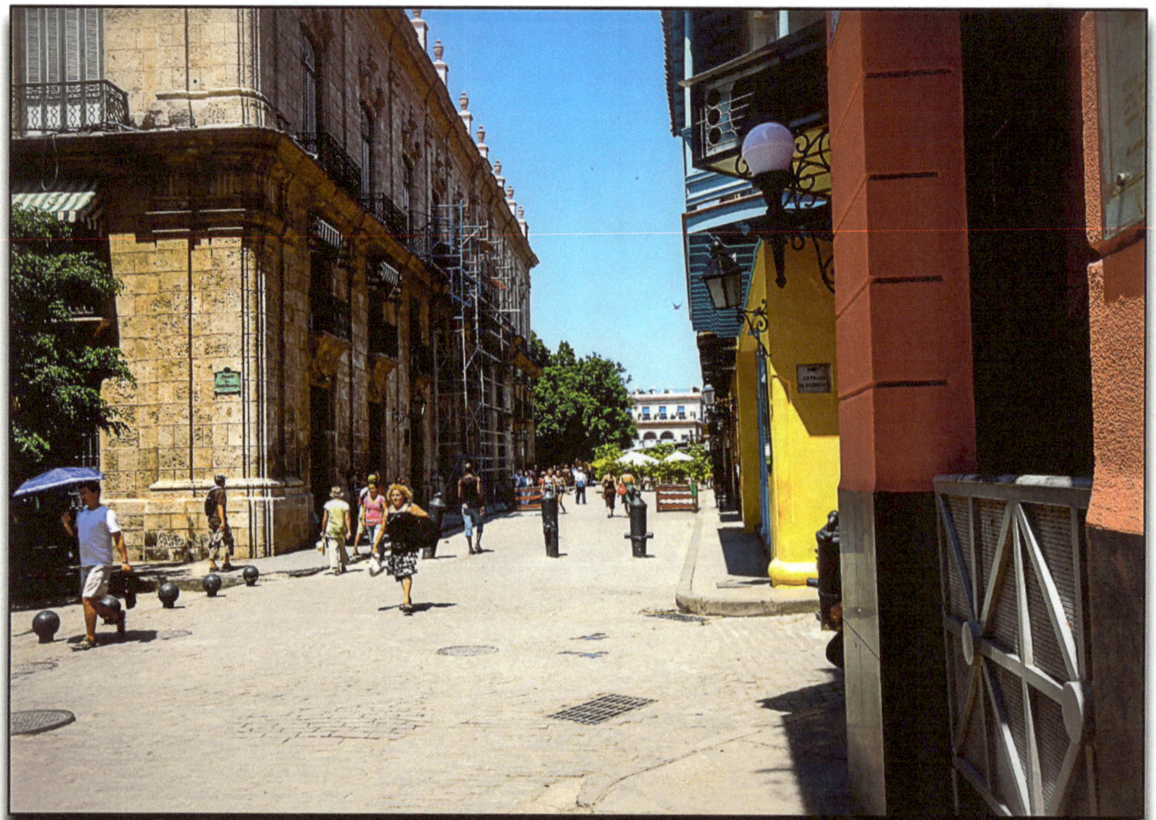

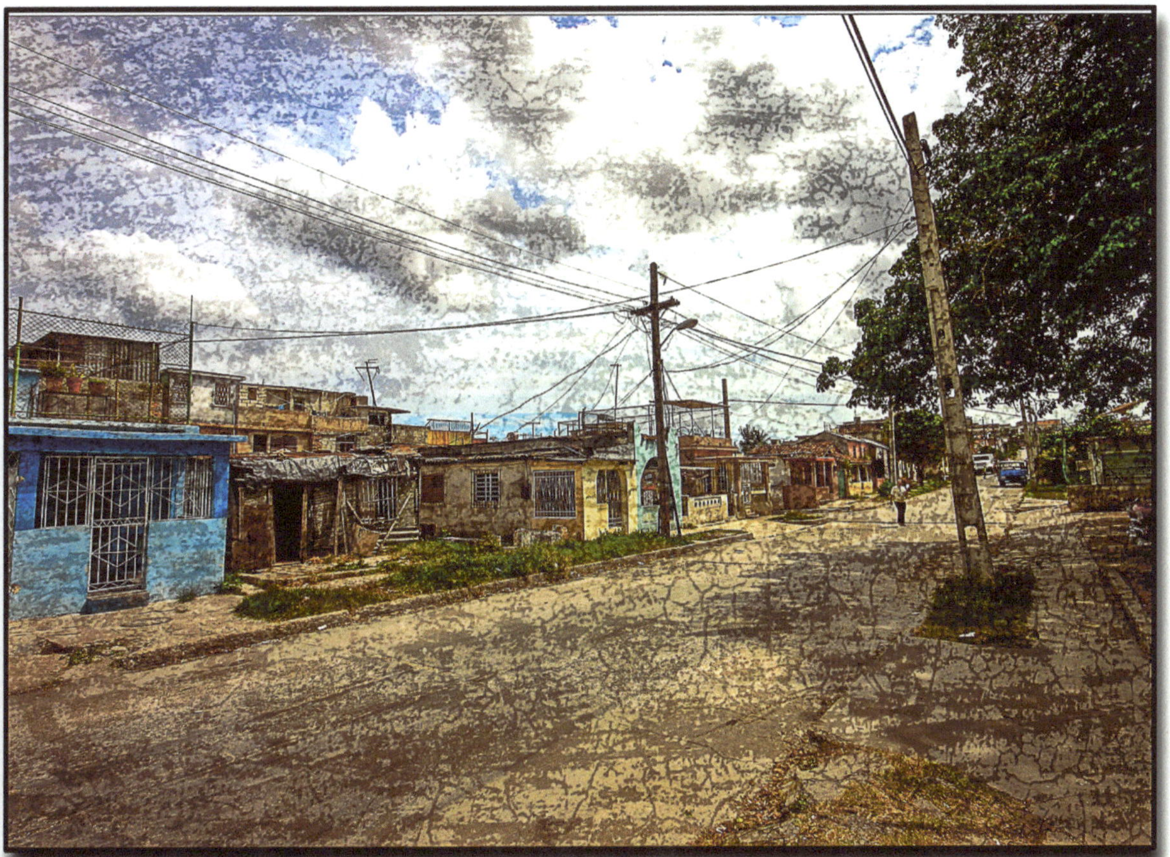

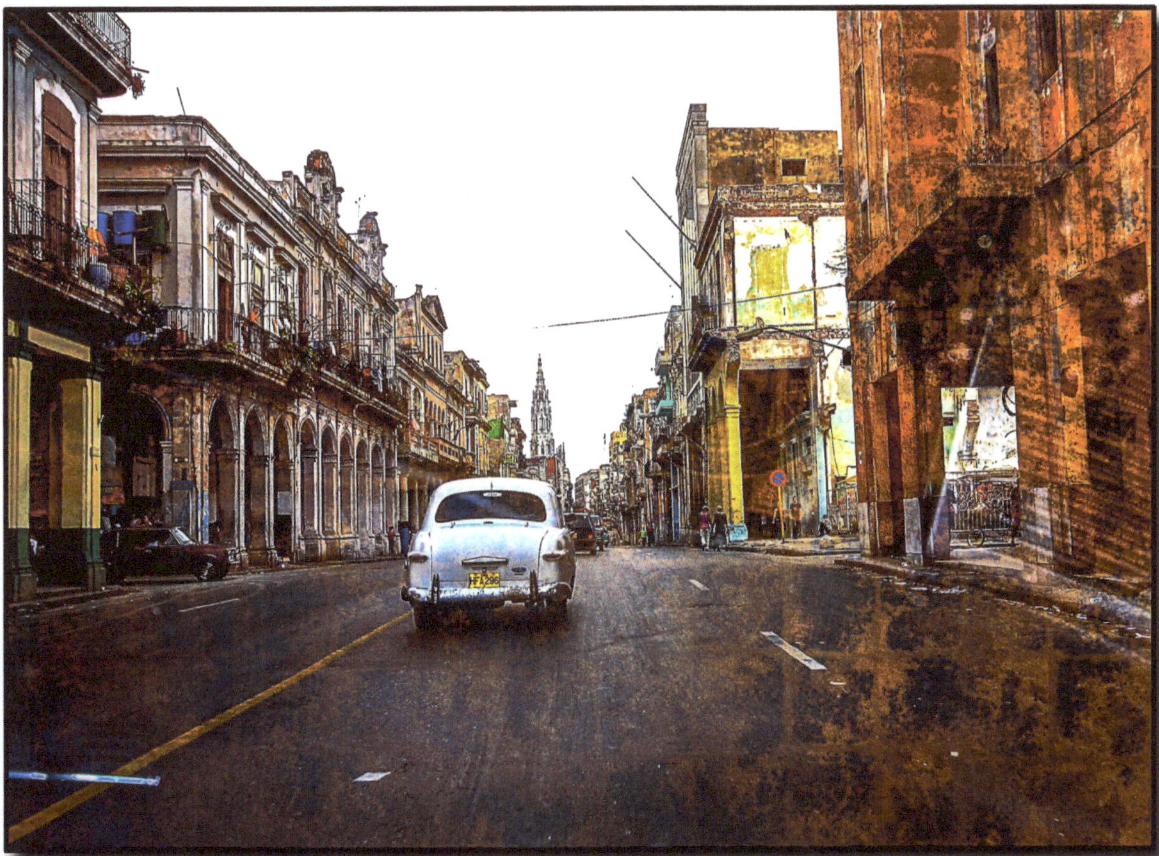

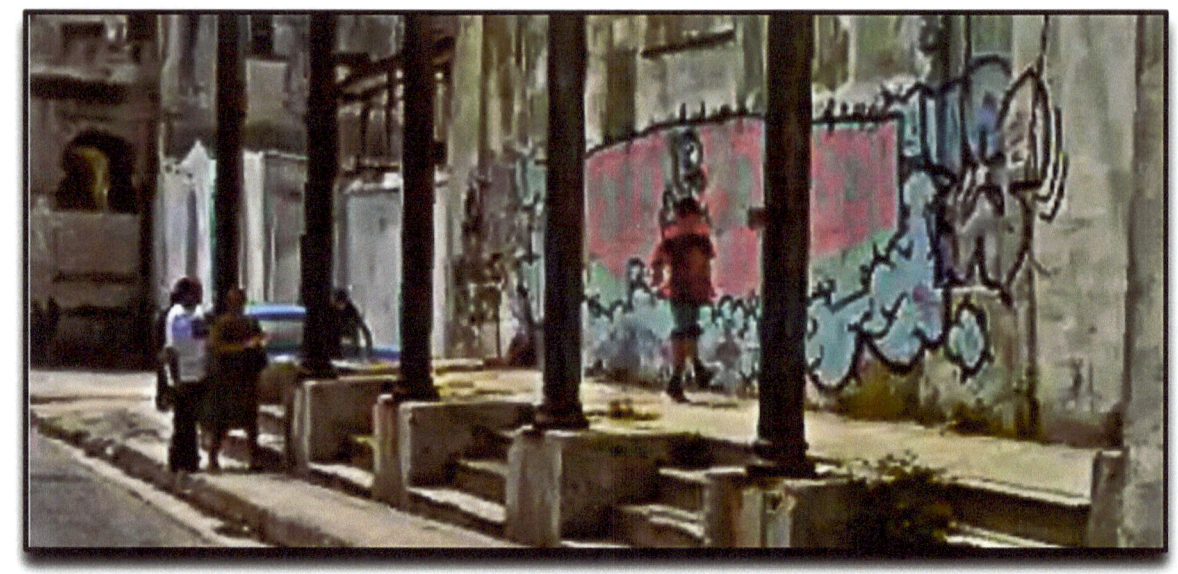

The Backside of Havana and the Lonely Planet.

Havana and Cuba in general have suffered decades of economic deterioration, especially since the 1991 collapse of the Soviet Union, its primary supporter. Many buildings have fallen in ruin though a number are being restored. The narrow streets of old Havana contain many buildings, accounting for perhaps as many as one-third of the nearly 3,000 buildings found in Old Havana. Following the revolution, Castro's revolutionaries took control of the Cuban economy. Factories were put under state management, farmland handed to cooperatives, and large houses and buildings were carved up into small apartments and doled out to the poor. Houses and property could no longer be bought or sold, only traded. In the inner-city municipalities of Old Havana and Centro Habana, as well as other poor neighborhoods many people are living under slum conditions.

There is a shortage of everything in Cuba. Helpful tips this traveler received before leaving for Cuba was to take indispensable essentials such a roll of toilet tissue, handy wipes, and mayonnaise and hot sauce if you like hotdogs and hamburgers. Sure enough, when I went to use the restroom at an Old Havana restaurant, there was someone outside the door selling sheets of tissue paper; and when I stopped for a hotdog at a local stand, all I got was a dry bun and meat. This was not all the time but frequent. Also, take as much money as you think you will need to spend--there are no ATM's for getting cash to convert to Cuban tourist dollars and they don't take credit cards.

The average monthly wage in Cuba as of July 2013 was 466 Cuban pesos, which are worth about 19-US dollars. Cuba has a dual currency system, whereby most wages and prices are set in Cuban pesos (CUP), while the tourist economy operates with Convertible pesos (CUC), set at par with the US dollar. To make an estimate about the cost of the life in Havana you have to take in account the cost of housing, electricity, water. These costs are in Cuba very low. Secondly there are the social benefits. With the ration booklet (the libreta) each Cuban family get a basic ration of staples such as rice, beans, cooking oil, salt, sugar and bread. They also get the following in limited quantities: 1 piece of soap, 1 toothbrush, and 1 tube of toothpaste. Milk is only available for mothers with children below the age of six.

Cubans are kept separate from the tourist by the two-currency system. Foreign currency is not accepted and must be converted for spending in Cuba. Most items above the basic needs are priced in tourist dollars, which is nearly 25 times that of the Cuban Peso. So you won't find Cubans spending in Tourist areas nor tourist spending or shopping in real Cuban areas--which are the back streets on downtown Havana (Old Havana). Tour buses are expensive and keep most Cubans off. Tour buses go to certain locations and are very confined. You have to be quite adventurous to see Cuba as it really is. In the photos that follow, you'll notice that there are no tourist, only locals in the neighborhoods and on the streets of the backside of Old Havana. The lighting is deem, streets not so clean. And most building and streets are in grave need of repair and upkeep. This is the lonely planet...everyday life in Cuba.

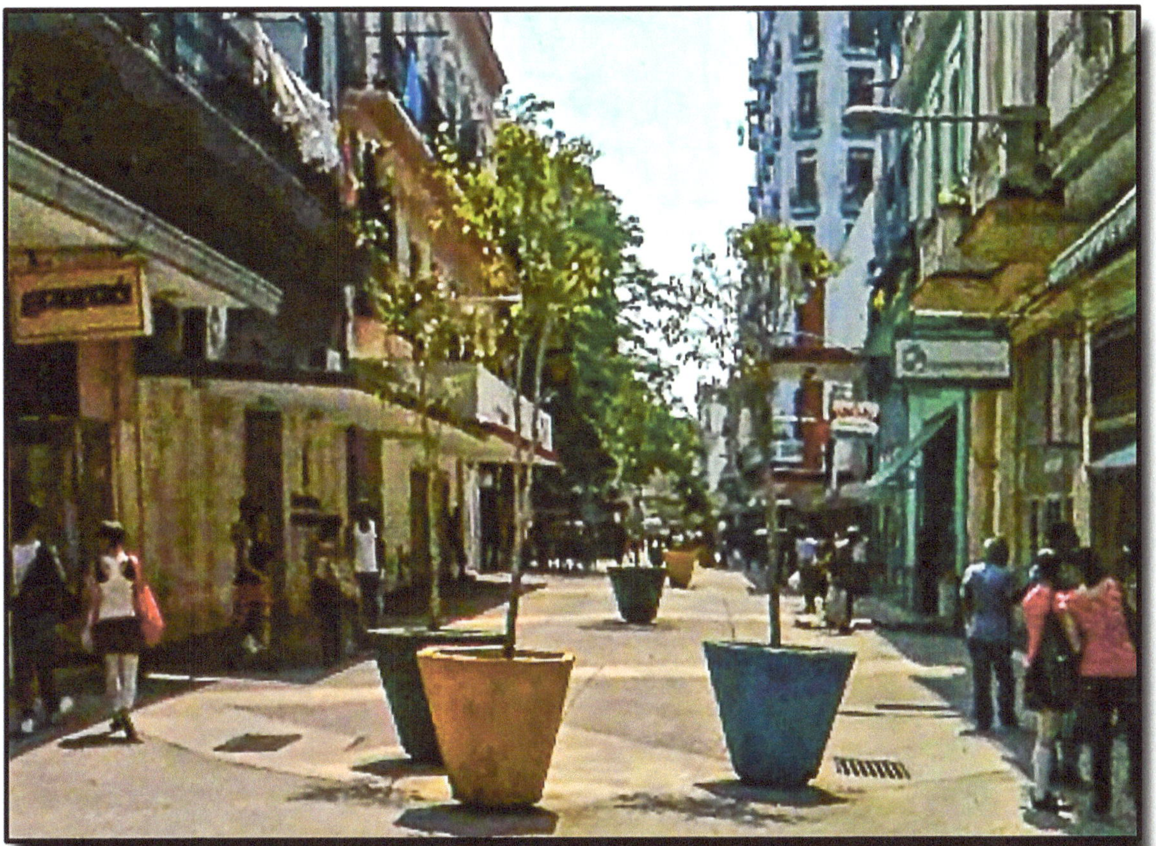

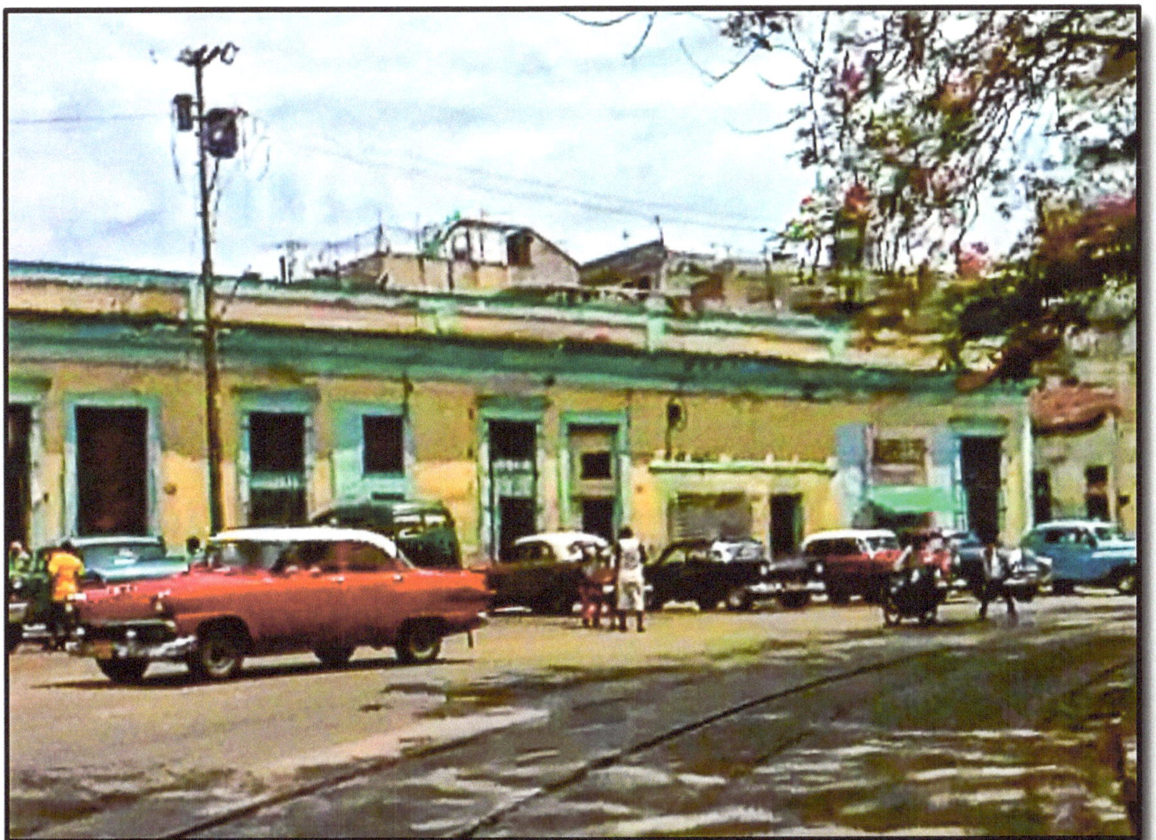

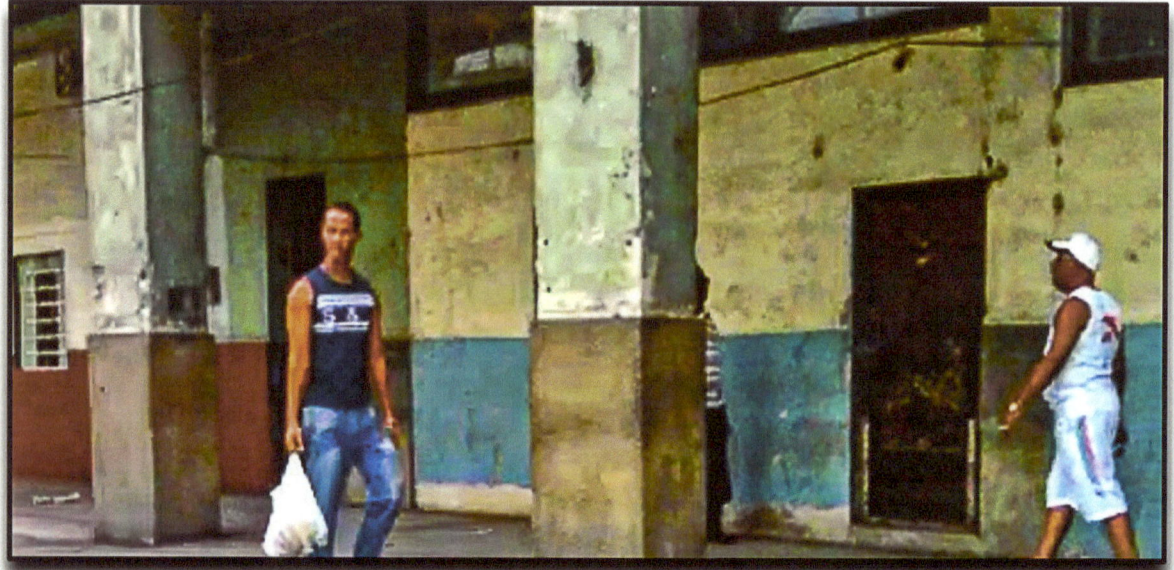

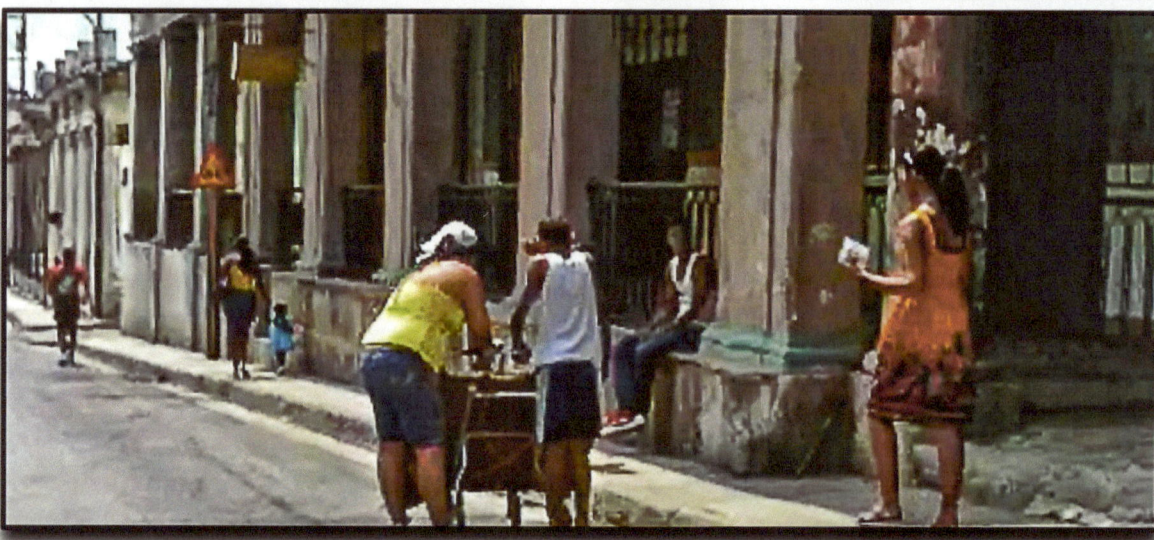

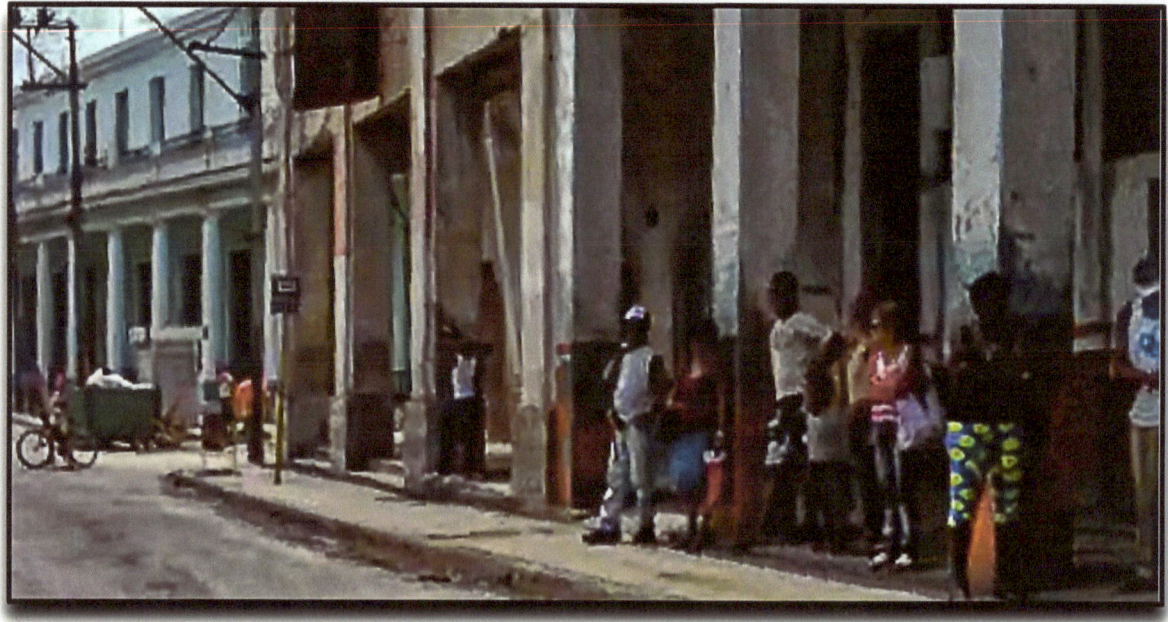

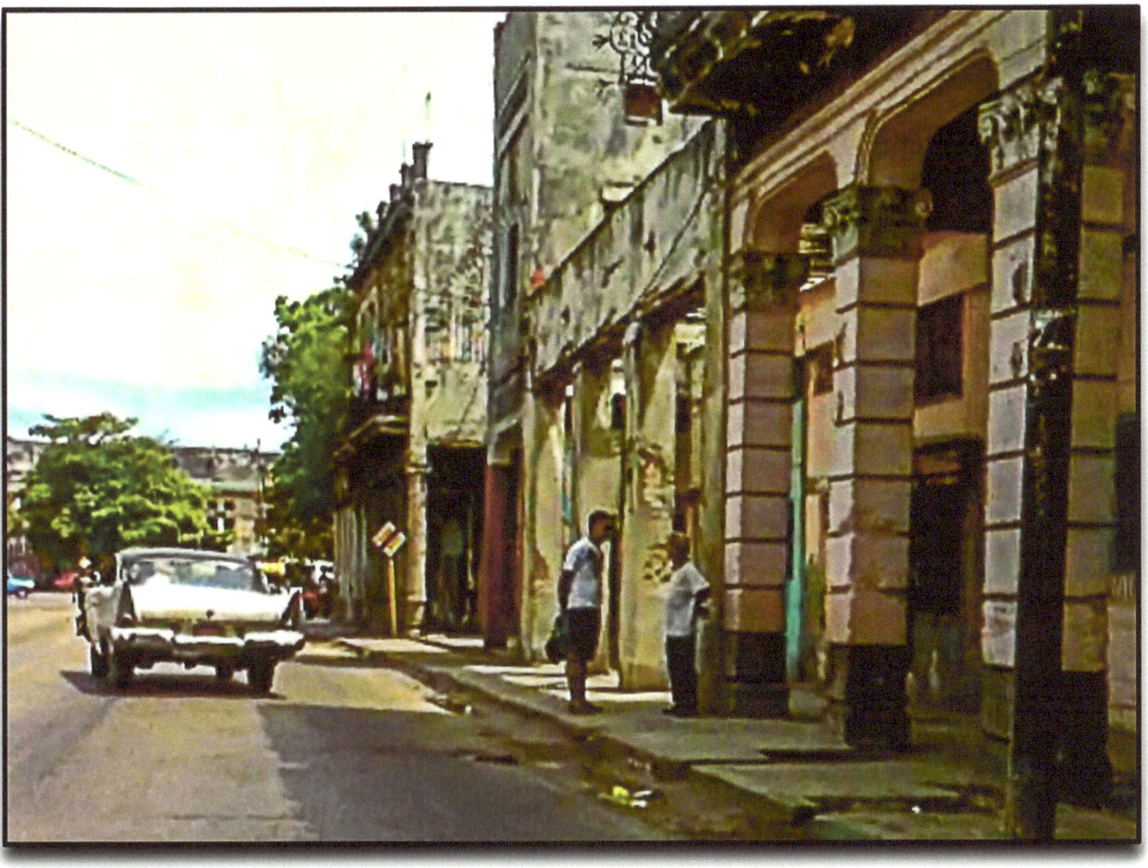

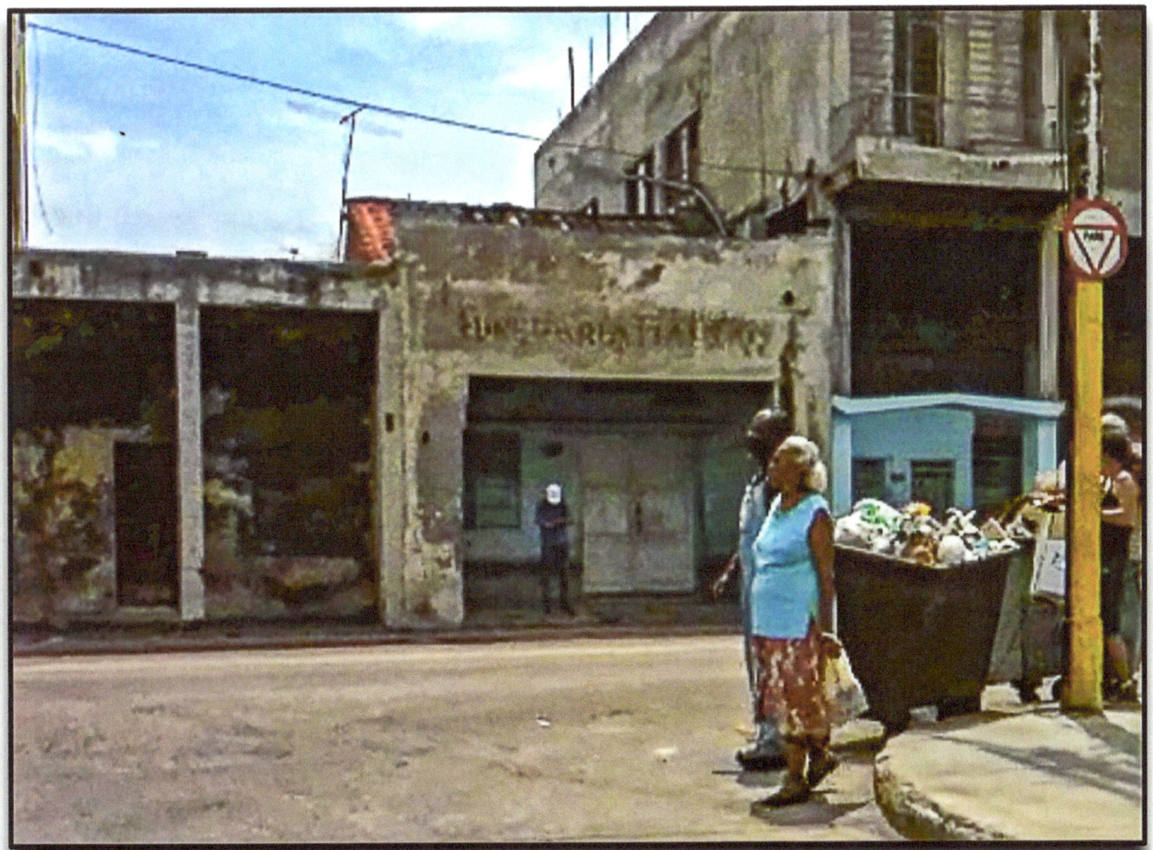

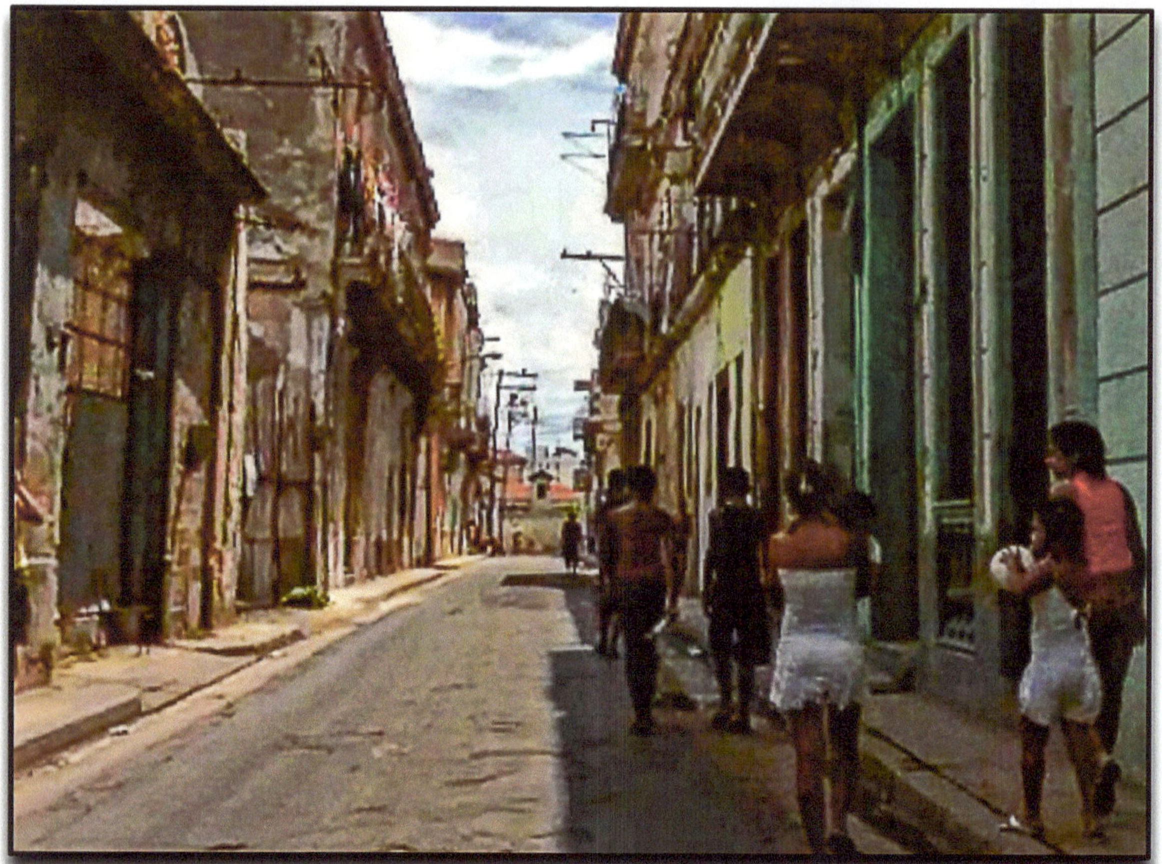

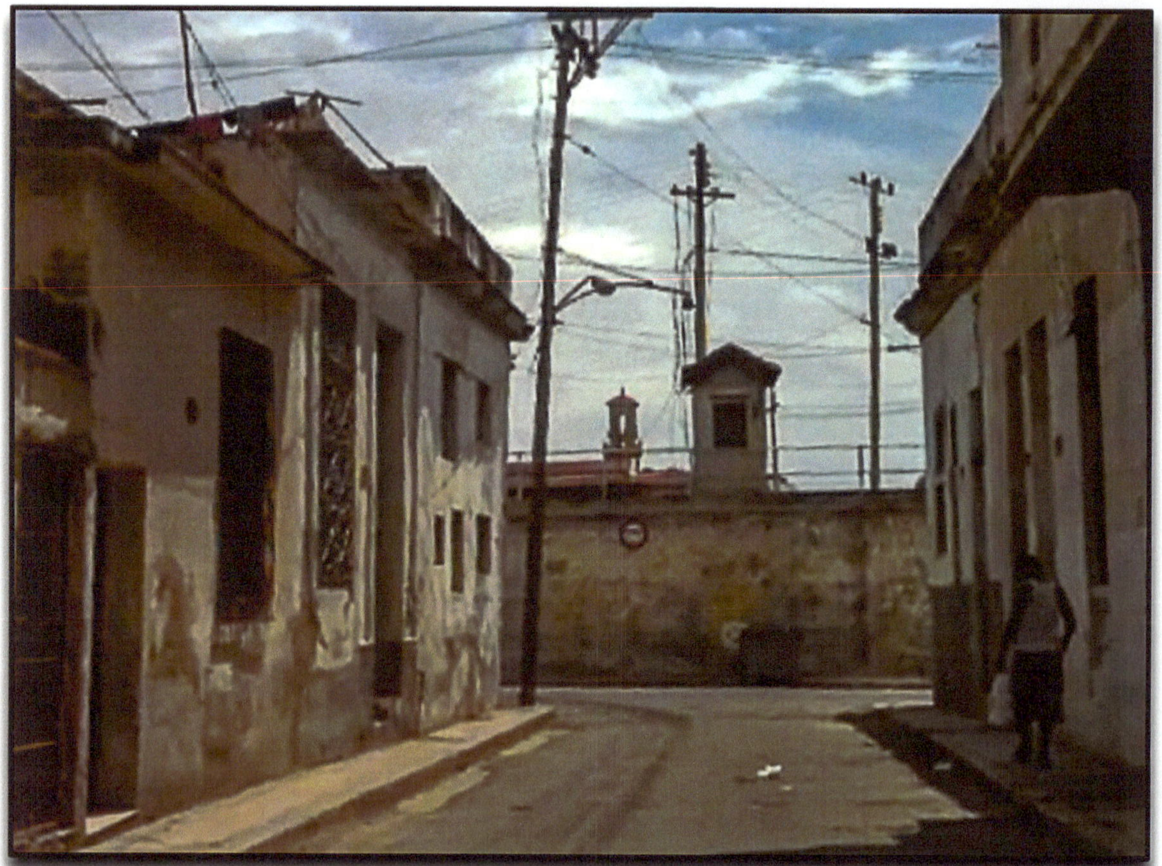

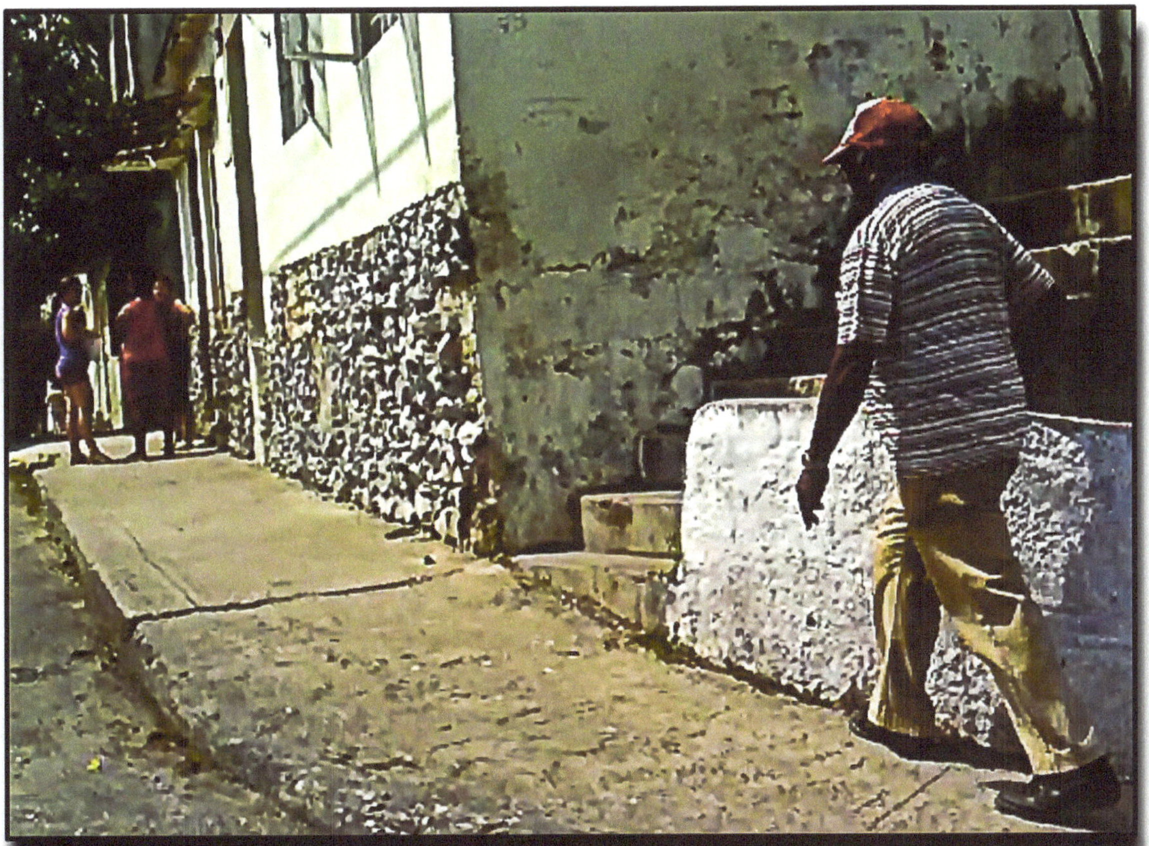

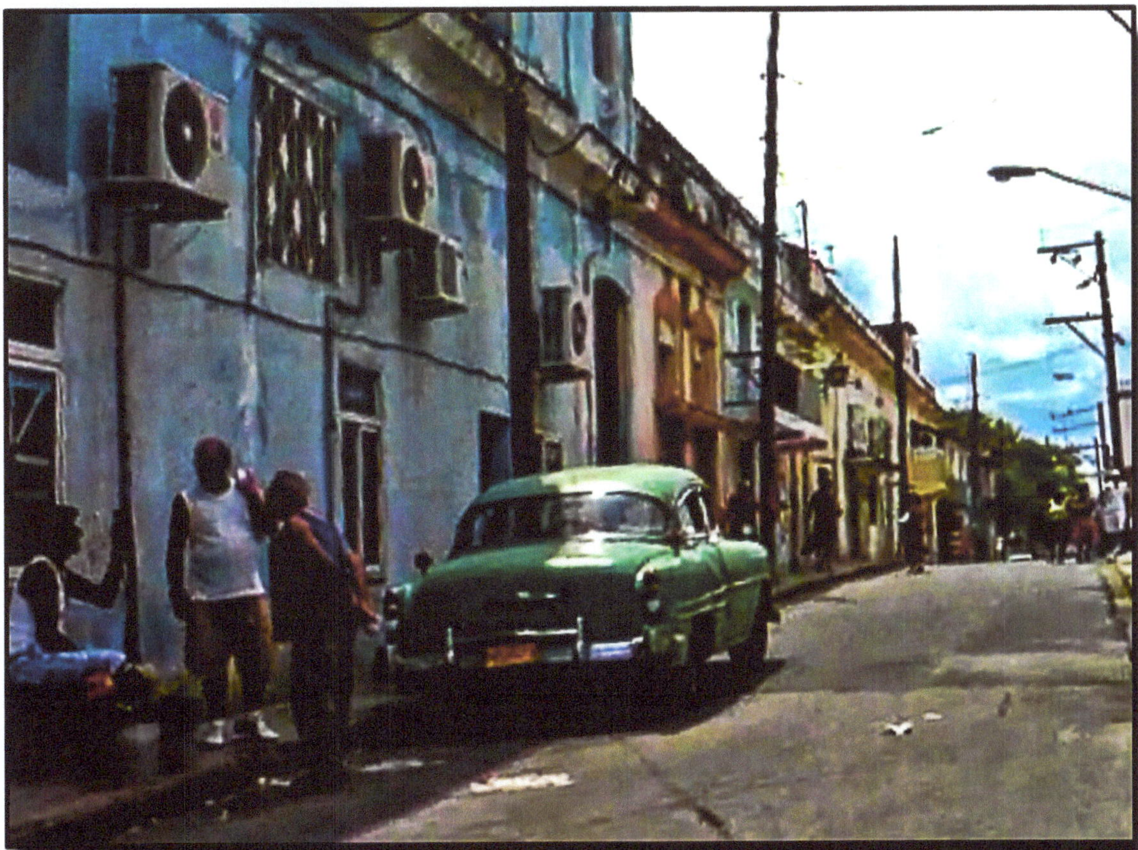

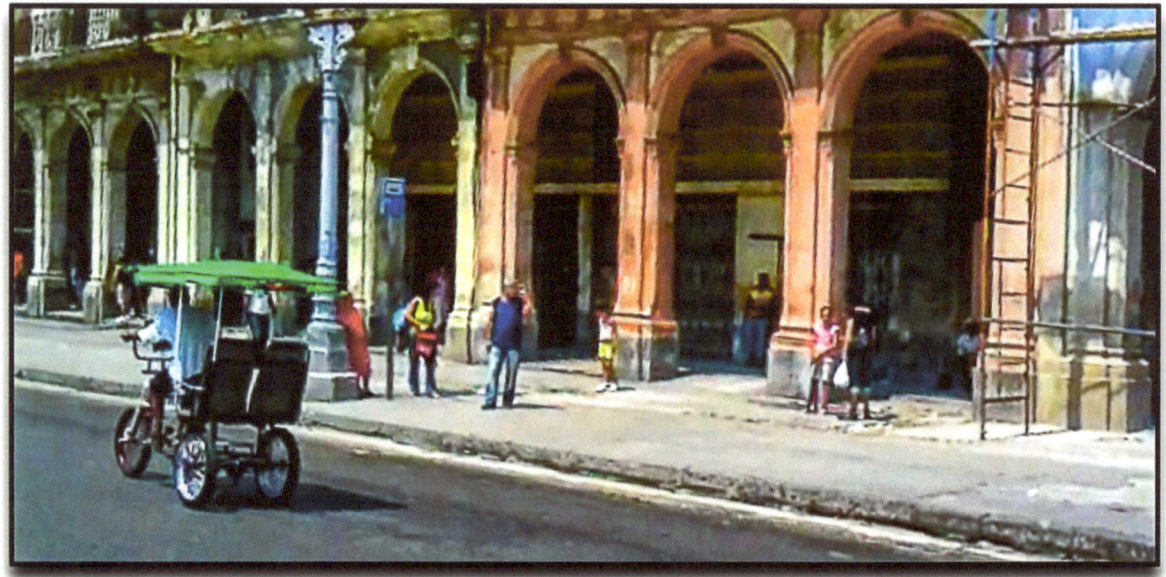

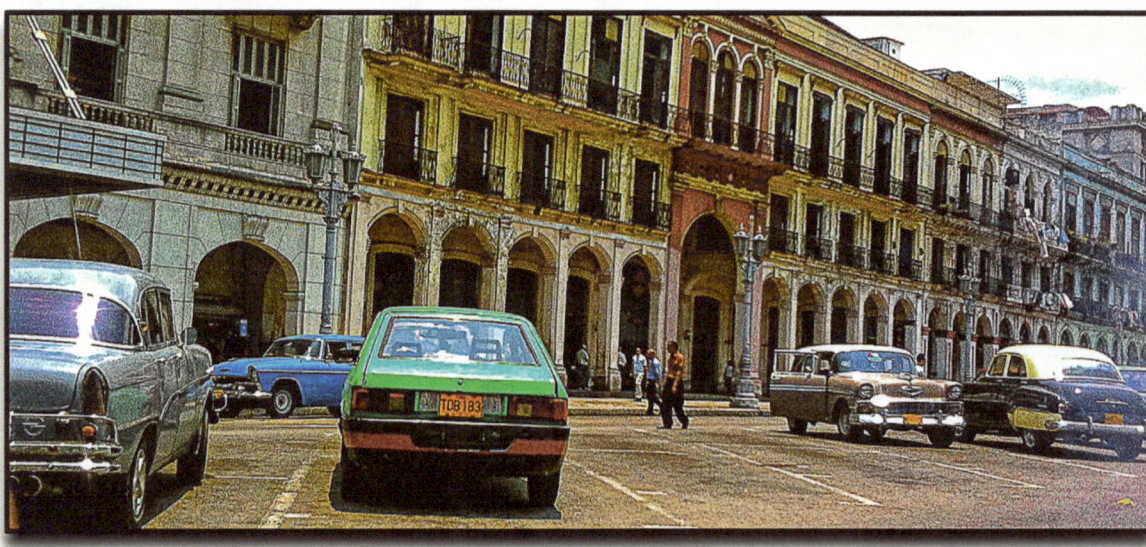

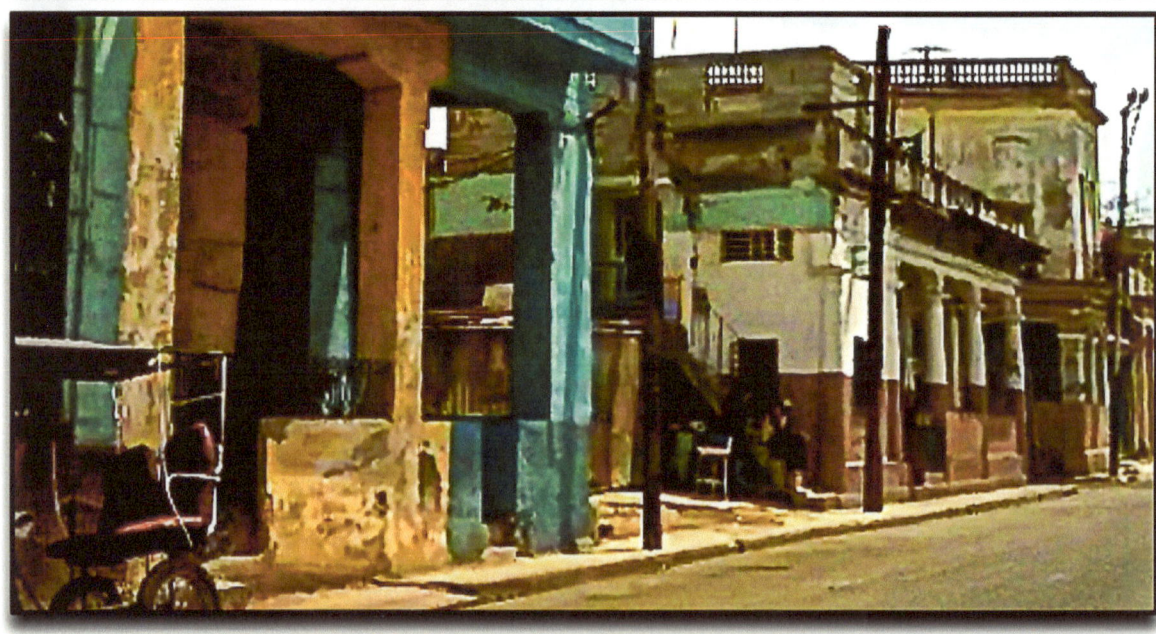

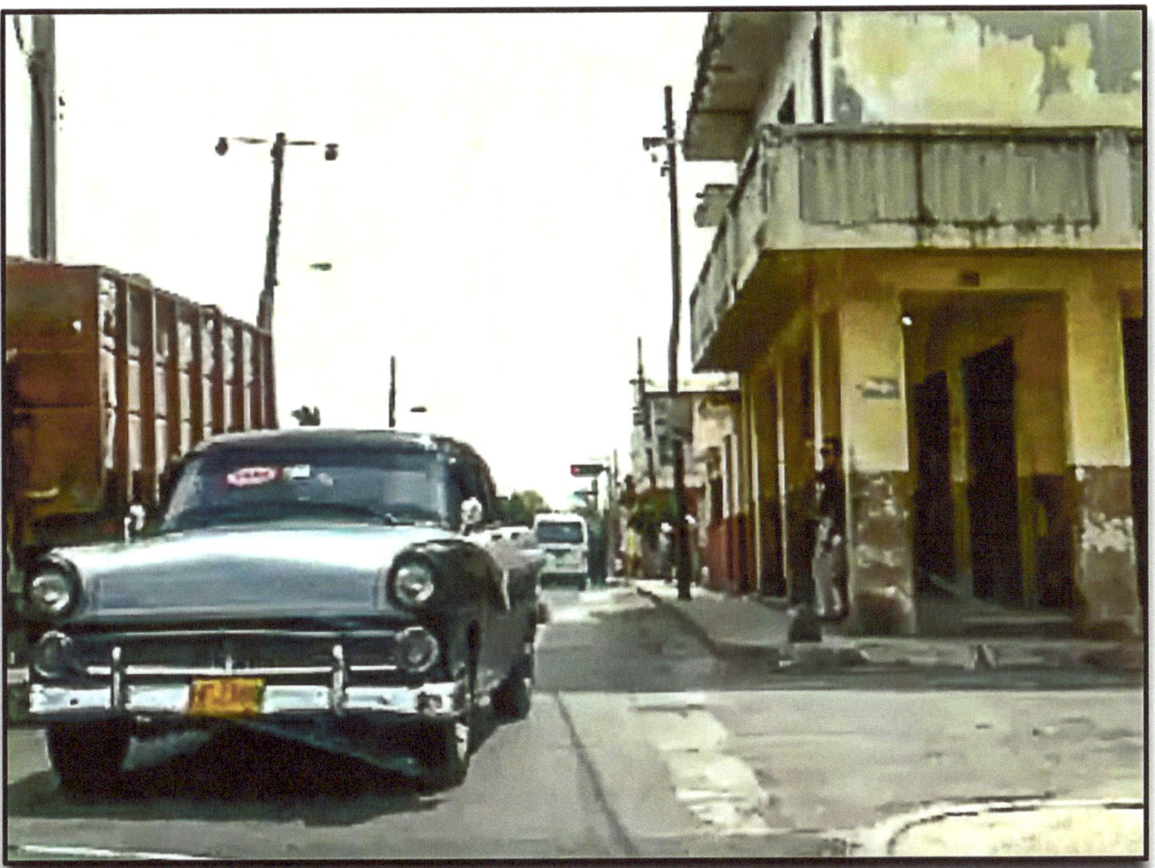

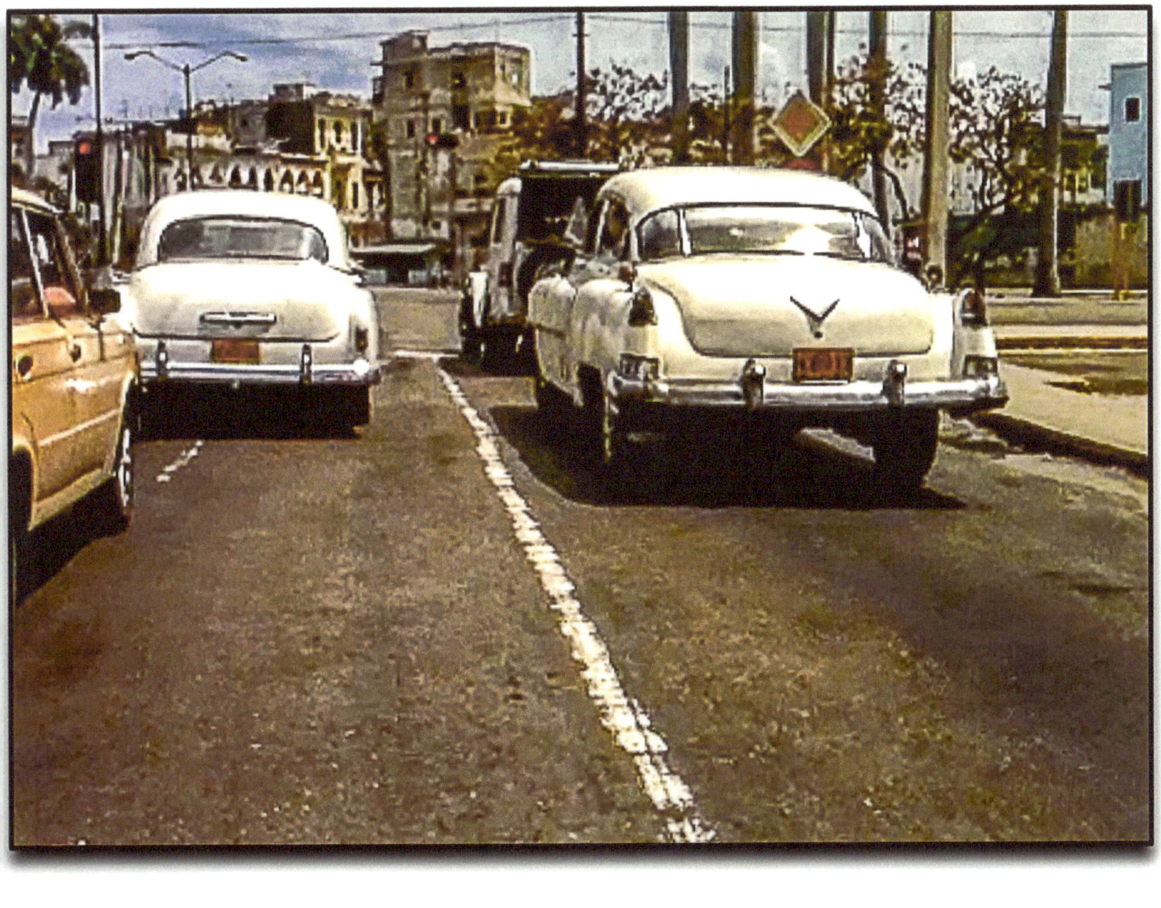

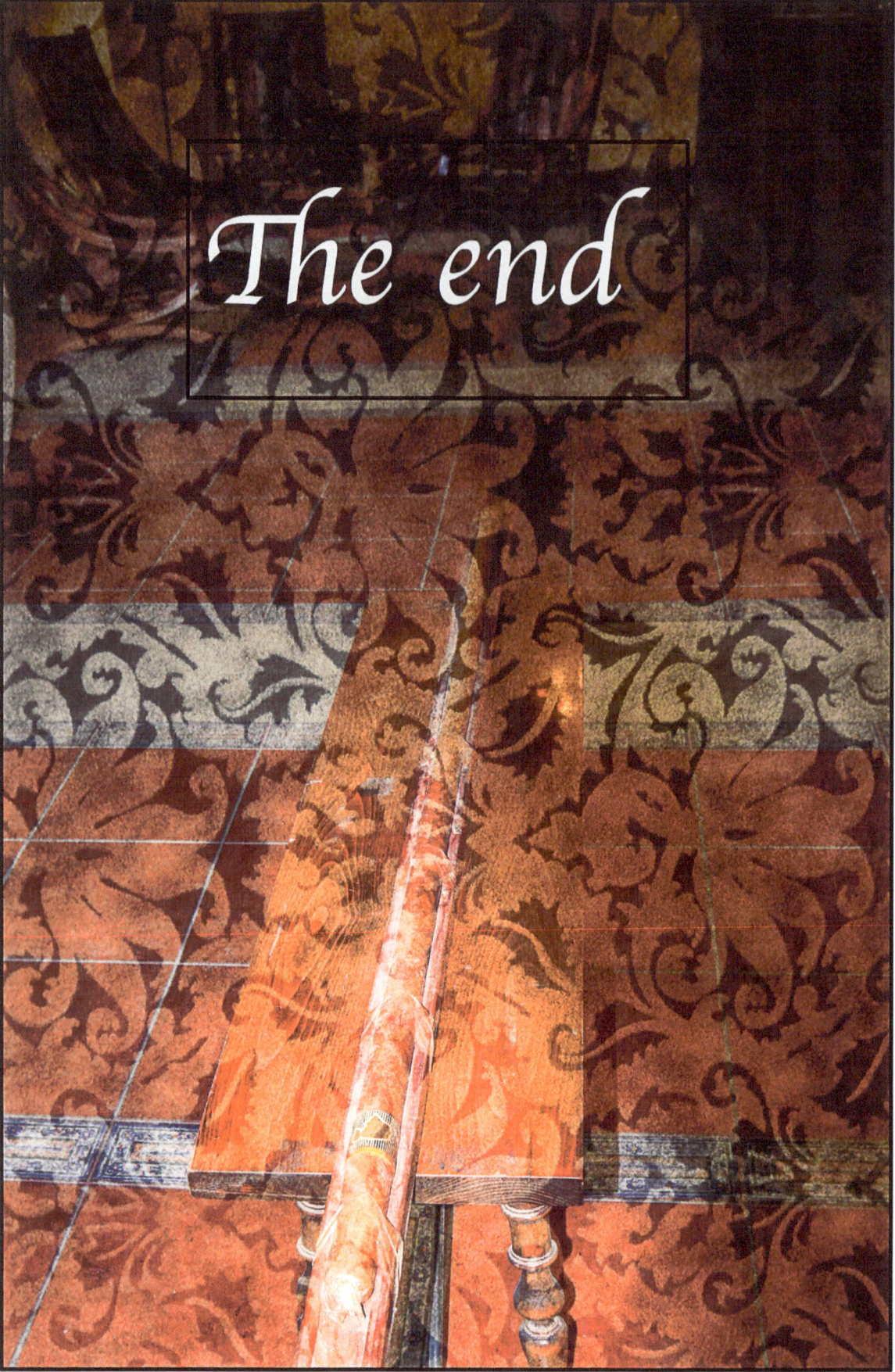

The end

www.ingramcontent.com/pod-product-compliance
Lightning Source LLC
Chambersburg PA
CBHW040750200526
45159CB00025B/1831